P9-EAX-483

Woman of Her Word: Hispanic Women Write

edited by
Evangelina Vigil

ARTE PUBLICO PRESS
Houston

JUN   '94

Riverside Community College
Library
4800 Magnolia Avenue
Riverside, California 92506

PS508.H57 W66 1987
Woman of her word : Hispani
women write

Second Edition, 1987

ISBN 934470-27-1
LC 83-072581
Copyright © 1983 *Revista Chicano-Riqueña*
PRINTED IN THE UNITED STATES OF AMERICA

CONTENTS

Prose

Criticism

Art

Introduction

The literature being produced by Latina writers represents a source of human intelligence that is new to literary audiences. Removed from the mainstream of American literature and barely emerging on the Hispanic literary scene, the creativity of Latina writers exists autonomously. Their literary products offer unique portrayals of the human experience from a woman's perspective. Through their work the writers affirm that, despite the double oppression that Latinas confront as women and as minorities in this country, their intellect and creativity flourish. It is often that conflict brought on by social alienation that works as a catalyst for creativity. The originality and unique literary contexts of the works featured in *Woman of Her Word* reflect the diversity of the Latin American cultures that the writers represent, including Mexican American, Puerto Rican, Cuban, Costa Rican and Chilean, among others.

Latina writers often portray the woman as a symbol of spiritual strength, virtue and wisdom. As a persona in the literature, the Latina is a woman of her word—*mujer de su palabra*. In this role, the Latina is self-sacrificing to her family as a mother and wife. She conveys values to her family members by way of example, and through the oral tradition, and, as such, she represents a tie to the cultural past. The woman is portrayed as the sensitive one in the family who expresses love and teaches respect for self and others. And, most importantly, she is the giver of life. Consequently, she knows pain: the pain of giving birth, the pain of losing a child, the pain of seeing her children suffer, the pain of isolation and alienation. As a human being empowered with the capability of performing the life-giving miracle, the woman as a symbol represents regeneration and the continuation of life. Thus, in the poem, "Woman-Hole," Carmen Tafolla utilizes the mother's womb as an all-encompassing symbol and source of knowledge, wherein lies the mystery of life:

> Some say there is a
>   vacuum—a black hole—
>   in the center of womanhood
>   that swallows countless
>   secrets and has strange
>   powers

In another poem entitled, "MotherMother," Tafolla personifies earth as the mother of all humanity who, with compassion, offers a universal lesson: respect for and the preservation of life. Referring to the tragic loss of life at Hiroshima, the poet imparts:

         . . . Now—
            That child is gone
            That cut is mended
            But let us
               save
                  the next

   That women learn social behavior from other women is a recurrent
theme in the literature. Young girls grow up very much as apprentices to
their elders, particularly to their grandmothers, as noted by Tey Diana
Rebolledo. In "Tía Ester," by Tawese O'Conner, for example, the
persona recalls the strength and virtues of a favorite aunt who gave her
and other children guidance through their adolescence:

   For she fed us always. She stuffed us.
   And she loved us. With each morsel of food,
   She instilled in us a deep love
   of goodness, of kindness, of innocence.
   Food and love were intermingled
   Forever
   In Aunt Esther's house.

Elders impart upon the young girls their wisdom, moral philosophies
and womanly advice. A strong bond among women is thus nurtured, as
exemplified in "No Mercy," by Sandra Cisneros. In this poem, the
speaker shares a sisterhood and expresses empathy towards her husband's former wives, having instinctively deciphered:

   you must've said
   something cruel
   you must've done
   something mean
   for women to gather
   all of their things

**In "Letter to Ilona from the South of France," Cisnero's speaker affirms
the existence of this womanly bond:**

   . . . . . .how do I explain a joy this elemental
   simple like your daughter's hand outlined in crayon.

   And yet I think you understand
   my first sky full of stars—
   you who are a woman—. . .

   Implicit in the literature is that women possess an extra-sensory
capability of perceiving truth beyond the obvious. This is a trait which
young girls inherit from their mothers and other female role models.

Through observation and cognitive learning, a girl develops this instinctive talent and learns how to utilize it in her dealings with other women and with men. With this sense thus developed, nothing can be concealed from a woman's discerning eyes and, as exemplified in "The So-and-So's," particularly a jealous woman. In this poem, the speaker detects "narry a clue," of her lover's other women, "save one or two." With poignancy and exquisite humor, Cisneros communicates the wrath of a jealous woman. "I will not out so easily/. . ./. . . and let them bleed," the speaker proclaims to her lover. Women's instinctive ability to decipher truth is also shown in "Del medio del sueño," by Yvonne Sapia, when the speaker reads her mother's wordless actions and senses her distrust:

> She glides in quietness to my dresser
> shifts the intimate fabrics around
> like fresh evidence.
> Del medio del sueño,
> I am not so far that I cannot come back
> to watch her wear down in purpose.

The Latina as a sensuous woman is another persona elaborated in the literature. This is significant in that it represents a breaking of the stereotype of the sexually inhibited woman. In "Casa," by Carmen Tafolla, the speaker admires her lover who "wears manhood like sunlight." In Sandra Cisneros' "Letter to Ilona from the South of France," the persona speaks of a release from inhibitions. She acknowledges that, whereas in the past she was one who feared "darkness," she has now overcome that fear:

> The night I let slip from my shoulders.
> To wander darkness like a man, Ilona
> My heart stood up and sang."

"Amor Negro," by Sandra María Esteves, likewise, affirms woman's femininity and romantic assertiveness. In this poem Esteves speaks of love and affection which reap physical and spiritual fulfillment and an appreciation for the beauty in life:

> we kiss and suck the delicate juice
> and sculpture flowers from the stone skin
> we wash them in the river by the moonlight
> with offerings of songs

In the creative space of the Latina writer, there often exists a reverence for nature. Their works are colored with imagery and metaphors relating to the planting and sowing of the seed and to roots too deep to be unearthed. Poems such as "Sugarcane," by Achy Obejas, and "Fresh Mint Garden," and "¿Sin Raíces Hay Flor?" by Cordelia

Candelaria, allude to the perennial cycle of life and nature which symbolizes human survival and spiritual and cultural endurance.

References to dreams abound in the literature as symbols of truth, vision and spirituality. Dreams may serve as premonitions and offer insight into the future, as exemplified in "Dreams by Appointment Only," by Silviana Wood. They may encompass the supernatural, as in "Alma-en-Pena," where a spirit appears to the protagonist in her sleep to reveal the identity of a murderer. Dreams are significant in that they uncover the psyche of the Latina, and Latina writers utilize them in their works as literary devices which allow the reader entry into the subject's stream of consciousness. Through dreams the subconscious is unveiled, as is the process of synthesis of information necessary for the formation of thought. In "Alma-en-Pena," Vallbona's protagonist reveals to her husband the following:

> . . . vos sabés. Isidoro, yo adivino que dentro de mí va cuajando algo en forma que no alcanzo a distinguir. Es como si todavía la distancia entre eso y yo fuera tal. que su imagen resulta imprecisa. A veces un pedazo de ese algo se aclara, pero como pasa con los rompecabezas complicados, después de juntar una pieza con otra, sólo veo una mancha negra, tal vez un esbozo de retina o la sombra de una nube del diseño total. . . .

Dreams often reveal the protagonist's repressed mental state and consequent alienation. In "Del medio del Sueño," by Yvonne Sapia, the persona states, "I am trapped somewhere/in the walls of my dream," and she makes reference to "the passing of nights which permit few easy exits."

The ritual of dance appears in the literature as a symbol of spiritual strength amid life's hardships. The performance of this ritual often expresses happiness and rejuvenation. As such, it represents a transcendence of the harsh realities that women and people in general confront daily. In "Bailando," by Pat Mora, the speaker notes the invincible spirit of her aunt:

> you, white-haired but still young
> waltzing on your ninetieth birthday,
> more beautiful than the orchid
> pinned on your shoulder,
> tottering now when you walk
> but saying to me, "Estoy bailando,"
> and laughing.

But holding the necessary "posture" of that dance is a strenous balancing act that not everyone can perform. Thus, in "Ten Dry Summers Ago," by Angela De Hoyos, the persona speaks of having "to dance, pivoting—as a Chicano would say/ en un daimito . . ." In "The Posture of the Dance," this ritual is presented as an affirmation of life. In this poem, the speaker notes that her mother's ability to perform this ritual is the miracle of life:

> For her legs do not speak
> nor hear the miseries
> of the long road to truth

In the poem, "Isleta," by Antonia Quintana Pigno, the dance ritual is presented in a religious context. As such it serves as a symbol of spirituality and affirms the survival of native religious beliefs. Referring to an ancient native ritual, the poet writes:

> In your center
> in the kiva
> the growing center of light
> beckons the dancers
> the dance begins.

The religious conflict faced by Latinas persists as a theme in the literature. In "Isleta," Pigno conveys the spiritual struggle of a people to maintain their native beliefs in a society which preaches and imposes Christianity:

> Año 1619
> In order to preserve the culture
> a command of Governor Eulate
> permits the people their ancient dances.
> Angered, Fray Salvador dons upon his head
> a crown of thorns
> and moves amongst the dancing
> islet people
> a heavy wooden cross across his shoulders.

In "The Broken Web," by Helena María Viramontes, religion is represented by God in the image of a man who has no understanding, and by the priest who is detached from the spiritual needs of those whom he confesses. The protagonist's conscience is haunted by a guilt instilled by the Christian belief of heaven for saints and hell for sinners. This sense of guilt reflects the Christian doctrine which teaches that woman is the bearer and transmitter of original sin. "You righteous cruel, cruelest bitch," the husband rages at his wife, recalling her unforgiveable sin of betrayal--her loss of virginity with another man. He continues:

> . . .Have I no right to be unfaithful? Weren't you? Vete mucho a
> chingar a tu madre, más cabrona que la chingada . . .

The rancor that he bears is the source of merciless vengeance:

> Rave, rave, you woman—you guiltness one? You, the very counterfeiter, you whorish bitch. Stay, sit, before I strike you again. And again; but you will not cry in front of me, will you? You will not please me by unveiling your pain, will you? Let them hear, they're probably not mine anyway.

In "Gloria, Salutación: Ave," Iliana Rivero makes bold use of poetic license in a sacreligious poem written in the form of a powerfully symbolic prayer reminiscent of the "Hail Mary." In this "prayer," woman denounces her subservience to man and God, whom she sees as one and the same. As in "The Broken Web," the woman makes a definitive break with tradition in order to free herself from the misery and burden of guilt imposed by man and God.

Evident in this literature is the traditional role in which the Latina frequently remains locked, a role imposed by her cultural upbringing, by her family, by males and society. Her's is a constant battle against repressive elements which, as Luz María Umpierre notes, breed anxiety and beckon the protagonist to seek changes. The break with these traditions is often the climax in the literary works.

Writers such as Nicholasa Mohr and Mary Helen Ponce point to racial prejudice as a major source of social conflict and alienation faced by Latinas and minorities in general. This confrontation is inherent in educational and social institutions which discriminate against minorities due to race, language and cultural beliefs. In "An Awakening," Mohr reveals the depravity of a segment of this country's population, whose mentality is literally written on the wall of a restaurant:

NO COLOREDS
NO MEXICANS
NO DOGS
WILL BE SERVED ON THESE
PREMISES

In "Recuerdo: Los Piojos," Ponce communicates the emotional and psychological trauma experienced by young children at the hands of racist school teachers. At a very tender age, minority children must learn to cope with the sometimes subtle and, at other times, blatant arrogance of prejudiced individuals.

Even in her own home, the Latina is confronted with repressive influences. In "Elena," by Pat Mora, the speaker is ridiculed by her husband and children when she tells them of her interest in learning to speak English. Ironically, she desires to educate herself not out of self interest:

> . . . Sometimes I take
> my English book and lock myself in the bathroom,
> say the thick words softly,
> for if I stop trying, I will be deaf
> when my children need my help.

Similarly, in "Dreams by Appointment Only," the protagonist's children and mother find it both surprising and amusing that she plans to enroll in college.

In the eyes of society and men in particular, intelligence is not necessarily a trait desirable in a woman. As noted by Iliana Rivero, in her poem, "El lugar que corresponde," a woman is considered by some males more attractive for her stereotyped image as a sexual object. Women's resentment of this sexist attitude could not be better expressed than in the words that Rivero directs to other women:

> y sabes
> que no escuchó ni una palabra,
> porque al fin son ideas de mujer
> que no hay por qué tomar en serio;
> porque sólo nos definen para el mundo,
> hermanita,
> dos pestañas oscuras,
> una boca entreabierta con gracia
> y unos pechos que desmienten (incluso hacen innecesaria)
> toda capacidad intelectual.

Sandra María Esteves, in her poem, "Transference," directs her commentary to males:

> So when you come to me, don't assume
> That you know me so well as that
> Don't come with preconceptions
> Or expect me to fit the mold you have created
> Because we fit no molds
> We have no limitations . . .

However, men as a rule do assume that they know women "so well as that." A number of assumptions which both men and women perpetuate by their dealings with each other are revealed throughout the literature:

One. A woman must remain in her place subservient to man. For a Latina this means her traditional role imposed by her own people, by man and society. In "Dreams by Appointment Only," as in "Elena," the woman's prescribed role is that of staying at home tending to the needs of the family. In "The Broken Web," the responsibility has become a burden for the protagonist and is the source of her depression:

. . . And she could not leave him because she no longer owned herself. He owned her, her children owned her, and she needed them all to live. And she was tired of needing.

As is reflected in the literature, women's dignity and sense of identity is often threatened. In "The So-and-So's," the persona's reaction to this kind of threat is straight forward: "I want to be like you. A who," she declares to her lover. But it is not that easy, as communicated in Angela De Hoyos' "Ten Dry Summers Ago," where she portrays a woman whose life-given job is that of fruitless plowing at external demands. At best, hers is an elusive sense of identity:

So now I have to landscape
this bare and godless ground
that keeps eroding
    into flyaway dust
        changing hands
            as easily as identity

In "Kimberle," by Achy Obejas, the woman is surrounded by hostile and oppressive elements which invite self-destruction and threaten not only her identity, but her very existence:

kimberle says no to the gods to the marble the
stones of the white heat that coarsens her veins
the system the muscular arms that hang low with
no purpose (an exile) perfect face imperfect
face kimberle is friends with a spectre a black
coat hands that mechanically tease at her neck
at her sex at the holes in her cheeks the sick
yellow dog eyes that respond with enchanted disease . . .

Two. A wife's place is in the home, whereas a husband's job and business outside of the home is a man's world. Thus, the protagonist in "The Broken Web," need not concern herself with what her husband does when he goes on business trips across the border. In "Alma-en-Pena," the husband is content to have his wife remain occupied with her household chores, while she is thoroughly bored and desires to become involved in civic activities. A spirit comes to her in her sleep and beckons her to reveal the identity of her murderer. This may be interpreted as symbolic of her active mind which once stimulated cannot be confined: ". . . qué putada! y que nadie la podía detener," the husband says of the protagonist in "Alma-en-Pena."

Three. Women must practice a tolerance in their relationships with men. Accordingly, the speaker in "The So-and-So's," is aware of her lover's other women, and to a point tolerates this, rationalizing, " but love is nouveau/ love is liberal as a general." In "The Broken Web," the protagonist resolves this dilemma through a tragic compromise.

Four. Man has a basic distrust for women. In "Alma-en-Pena," for a moment, the husband's fears mount as he conjectures that maybe his wife has inherited the insanity and criminal predisposition of her mother:

> . . . estará de veras loca? Tiene una mirada singular, como miraba su madre por aquellos días, cuando asesinó al padre en un arranque de locura. ¡Qué güevonada!, era una mujer suave, mansa, callada, de manos fláccidas sobre el regazo—como en un interminable reposo—y ojos llenos de distancias y vacíos. Pero un día se hichó de furor y mató al marido con el cuchillo de cocina. Quién quita que la haya confundido con un tierno lomito de res. Nina presenció el crimen desde un rincón, ¡la pobre! ¿Hay algo de extraño que después ella también se vuelva loca?

In "The Broken Web," the husband's distrust of his wife is a curse which bears hate and vengeance:

> Ha. Ha. That I, you say, am unfaithful to you? In Tijuana, last week? I should have spied on you that night you let him rip the virginity out of you, the blood and slime of your innocence trailing down the sides of his mouth. You tramp.

The focus of many Latina writers is on how women deal with the negative elements which persist in their unique, private worlds. Negative confrontations may lead the protagonist to positive reaction, as exemplified in Judith Ortiz Cofer's, "What the Gypsy Said to Her Children," where the power of invention and creativity in dealing with life's day-to-day social encounters is communicated. In this poem, the gypsy speaks of a transcendence of the human hatred and depravity which racism breeds:

> where all colors blend into one
> we will build our cities of light,
> we will carve them
> out of the granite of their hatred,
> with our own brown hands.

However, at times these negative influences can mount to a breaking point, and push the protagonist into negative recourses which may result in the demise of her antagonist and in serious repercussions for her. In "The Broken Web," for example, the protagonist destroys that which is the cause of her misery, and she must pay for her action:

15

. . . She would become a cricket wailing nightly for redemption. That suited her, she would be wailing for redemption. With the strength of defiant resignation, she stared, wide-eyed and zombie-like at the name printed on the wristband.

In "A Landlord's Dream of Hell," by Yvonne Sapia, the persona, "irreversible in her desperation," stabs the landlord—a likely target in the eyes of a tenant overcome by the hellish poverty which surrounds her. She, too, will have to pay her social debt for this criminal act. In these works the writers pose a universal moral question: Is killing that which is killing you a justifiable act of self defense? Is it an act forgiveable in the eyes of God and society? The answer is a judgement which lies in the conscience of the reader.

Pronounced in the literature, particularly in works by writers from Latin America, is a strong awareness of the historical political strife of third world peoples. Margorie Agosin, in her poem, "Estados Unidos," speaks of the cultural genocide of Latin American peoples at the hands of the capitalist oppressor:

Aunque confiésate
que gozabas de la triste enfermedad
de los pueblos mansos
y trepaste hasta la vía andina
para llenarte de cobres, cromosomas, de fusil
pero pensándolo bien. . . .

The poet alludes to scenes in Nicaragua, El Salvador and Chile, acknowledging the capitalistic "ready-made" culture which, ironically, has permeated into the lifestyle of the people of Central America. But these visible signs are deceiving, Agosin notes:

y todos vestimos botas de Cowboy
en un sordo diálogo de Rock and Roll.

Implicit in this statement is that, to the extent that acculturation has occurred, the penetration of U.S. culture into Latin American society is only on the surface and remains void of true meaning.

In "¿Dónde Están," Agosin speaks of "los desaparecidos"—those who have disappeared, noting the silent presence of a race of people that endures oppression and survives:

Yo juro ser la palabra
pero nunca lamentar a los
muertos que hoy y siempre
están.

That the oppressor eliminates not only human lives, but suppresses spiritual and intellectual freedom as well is the focus in Naomi Lockwood

Barletta's poem, "En el norte." Here the poet alludes to her native land where the beauty of the mountains and abundant vegetation sustain life and nourish creativity. This she contrasts with the indifferent, lifeless surroundings of the city which methodically extinguish creativity, silencing its victims:

Mis palabras aquí se mueren
como muere mi pueblo
sílaba por sílaba
hasta llegar a ser silencio
y nada más.

The most significant revelation in this anthology is the vibrant imagination, talent and intelligence of Latina writers, as unveiled through their works, and their apparent motivation to expand their personal world of human understanding. Clearly, as exemplified by the writers themselves, the role of the Latina that is being projected in this literature is one of action, assertiveness and invention. In her modern role the Latina is a doer. She is an active participant in shaping her life and destiny. The vitality, passion and positive determination of a woman who makes decisions instinctively, independently and confidently is communicated by Sandra Cisneros in "Love Poem #1." For the speaker in this poem, there is no vacillation, as she sets out to explore life's challenges and reap its rewards:

we are
connoisseurs
and commandoes
we are rowdy
as a drum
not shy like Narcissus
nor pale as plum

To the person who wishes to share with her a life of fulfillment and creativity, the speaker in Sandra María Esteves' poem, "Transference," consciously protective of her autonomy and identity, proposes:

Come in a dialogue of we
you and me reacting, responding
being something new
Discovering

In her solace, in that creative space profound, the Latina writer sculpts with words her artistic product. In her activated mind, creativity is sparked and intelligence breeds, compelling her to continue her artistic quest: "When will creativity cease to be child?", Esteves questioningly concludes, acknowledging the infinite capacity of the mind and the insatiability of the human spirit that desires more. So much more.

Self Portrait   *Patricia Rodríguez*

No Mercy

Your wives left
without a trace
both of them

they plucked
their long hair
from the kitchen sink
did not forget the ring
nor the domestic combs
not one stray stocking
did they leave

not a fingerprint

nor a subscription
to a favorite magazine

they fled

gathered their feathers
and bobby pins and string
left nothing

took their towels
and their initials
one child
expensive shoes

and vamoosed

without a clue

you must've said
something cruel
you must've done
something mean
for women to gather

all of their things

The So-and-So's

Your other women are well-behaved.
Your magnolias and Simones.
Those with the fine brave skin like moon
and limbs of violin and bones like roses.
They bloom nocturnal and are done
with narry a clue behind them.
Narry a clue. Save one or two.

Here is the evidence of them.
Occasionally the plum print
of a mouth on porcelain.
And here the strands of mermaids
discovered on the bathtub shores.
And now and again, tangled in
the linen—love's smell—
musky, unmistakeable,
terrible as tin.

But love is nouveau.
Love is liberal as a general
and allows. Love with no say so
in these matters, no X nor claim nor title,
shuts one wicked eye and courteously
abides.

I cannot out
with such civility.
I don't know how to
go—not mute as snow—
without my dust and clatter.
I am no so-and-so.

I who arrived deliberate as Tuesday
without my hat and shoes
with one rude black tatoo
and purpose thick as pumpkin.

One day I'll dangle
from your neck, public as a jewel.
One day I'll write my name on everything

as certain as a trail of bread.
I'll leave my scent of smoke.
I'll paint my wrists.
You'll see. You'll see.
I will not out so easily.

I was here. As loud as trumpet.
As real as pebble in the shoe.
A tiger tooth. A definite voodoo.
Do not erase me.

Let me bequeath
a single pomegranate seed,
a tell-tale clue.
I want to be like you. A who.

And let them bleed.

Sandra Cisneros

Love Poem #1

a red flag
woman I am
all copper
chemical
and you an ax
and a bruised
thumb.

unlikely
pas de deux
but just let
us wax
it's nitro
egypt
snake
museum
zoo

we are
connoisseurs
and commandoes
we are rowdy
as a drum
not shy like Narcissus
nor pale as plum

then it is I want to hymn
and halleluja
sing sweet sweet jubilee
you my religion
and I a wicked nun

Sandra Cisneros

Letter to Ilona From the South of France
for Ilona Den Blacken Nesti

Ilona, I have been thinking
and thinking of you since I went away,
dragging you with me across the south of France
and into Spain. Then back again.

I ran away to an island off the coast of Spain—
tiny jewels of fields beneath the jewel of sky—
and lost myself one night in crumpled poppies.

Odd for such a city poet like me
to find such comfort in the dark—
I who always feared it—and yet
I loved the way it wrapped me like a skin.

All those stars, Ilona. And wind.
Field illumined by those poppies.
Yes, that was good.

I wanted to bring that back forever,
wrap it in a velvet cloth to show you.
The wind from Africa. The field of poppies.
The way my bicycle hummed the distance.

And for me, Ilona, who has never known
the liberty of darkness, who has never
let go fear, how do I explain a joy this elemental,
simple like your daughter's hand outlined in crayon.

And yet I think you understand
my first sky full of stars—
you who are a woman—
the wind from Africa, the field of poppies,

the night I let slip from my shoulders.
To wander darkness like a man, Ilona.
My heart stood up and sang.

Woman-Hole

Some say there is a
  vacuum—a black hole—
    in the center of womanhood
      that swallows countless
        secrets and has strange
          powers

Yo no sé de'sas cosas
  solo sé que the
    black echo is music
      is sister of sunlight
        and from it
          crece
            vida.

Soulpain

They ask
    what it is like
        to lose
           a baby.

Seven hours later
    they are gone
        and I am here

        still trying
           to
        mouth
    an answer.

Eyesmute
Roomempty
I pull my body slowly to salute
Shiverstanding I proclaim in dry dead throat:

A part of my
        body
has been amputa-   And no one else
        -ted   can
                                    tell;

The seedlings of my
        soul   And the roots
have been ripped   out   tossed into   a
                                      grave.

MotherMother
(they see Hiroshima and speak of nuclear "defense")

Earth—
    Your womb has been
        cut open
            just as mine
            just as my mother's

    Your child has died
        in its halo of innocence
            just as mine
            just as my mother's

    Your heart has pounded
        angry, crying beats
            in slaughtered grasps
                for the child . . .
                    for your
                        soul

        and drummed slowly
            by the gravesite
                in time to the warm pulse
                    of the rocking wind
                        which lulls
                            the child's
                              tomb.

Now—
    That child is gone
      That cut is mended
      But let us
        save
            the next.

Casa

The comal smells like flour tortillas
   even when it's not
The jardín de hierba (casi) buena grows
    como si fuera éste cualquier barrio mexicano
    ni fijándose de los rednecks
The wildflowers (mojadas) cross over (sin papeles)
    and move in with us.
Y de pronto aparecen mil chamaquillos de la vecindad
    growing like arbolitos
    in our front yard

You wear manhood
   like sunlight.
And mi vientre (¡maceta chiflada!)
   se hincha
     queriendo, como las ciruelas
        del árbol
      cargar semilla
        también.

Father and Child   *Sandra María Esteves*

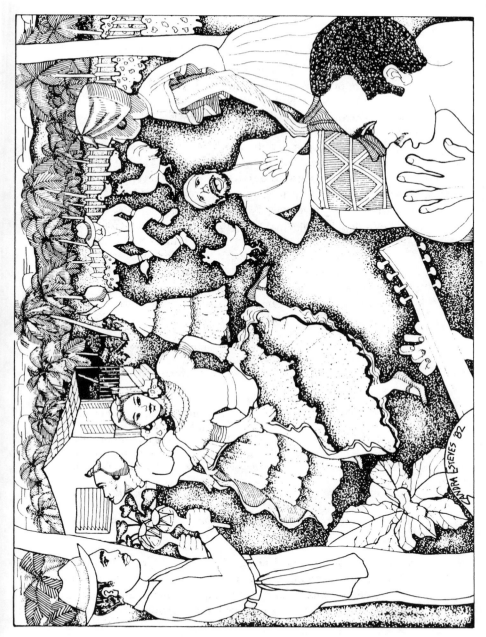

Música Indígena Puertorriqueña   *Sandra María Esteves*

Amor Negro

in our wagon oysters are treasured
their hard shells clacking against each other
words that crash into our ears
we cushion them
cup them gently in our hands
we kiss and suck the delicate juice
and sculpture flowers from the stone skin
we wash them in the river by moonlight
with offerings of songs
and after the meal we wear them in our hair
and in our eyes

A Celebration of Home Birth
November 15, 1981
for Yaasmiyn Rahiyma

Sometimes there is steam in the apartment
Thanksgiving was spent warm
We forget about some things in the heat
Listen to and play music, dreaming in dawn
Then it gets cold
Again the water freezes
The sink fills with dirty dishes
We seek escapes, find new warmths

4:30 a.m.: A tightening in my belly
Different from the others days before
This one electric, piercing blood
Five and Ten seconds long
Longer, growing stronger
I massage my belly fire
With thumbs forefinger and palm
The friction relaxes

5:30 a.m.: Juan paces with me
Heaving puts on his pants to make a list
Call the police, no, yes, no
Call the hospital, no, yes, no
Call the doctor, heavens no!

6:30 a.m.: The water breaks, we call the midwife
A rush of clear warm liquid down my legs
Socks and floor wet
Bed and towels soaked
Belly tightens longer
Growing stronger

7:00 a.m.: Two midwives arrive
At four centimeters I cannot sit still
Take a shower and prepare my body
Contractions grow in power, legs shake
Breathing with energy the birth force overwhelms me
Swept away on a powerful crest in the great ocean
No longer in control of my physical

The waves deepen and stretch
A whirlwind pulls me into its gravity
Warm liquid rushing out on each undulation
Blessing and bathing the house
A preparation
Rivers from my womb evolving the life spirit
I walk from room to room
Invoking assistance from the Angels of Birth

9:00 a.m.: It is time to push
I call to God feeling the burning release
As her head and body emerge from the darkness
As sacred as Sunday morning in winter
On my belly she screams for life
I pray for blessings
Give thanks to my Santos
Continue on the day.

Sandra María Esteves

Portraits for Shamsul Alam

Every morning when the sun rises
We stand in the light, capture
The warm heat to begin
The day with power, stirred with energy
We path a golden way, full of lifehood
Spirit laying seed for each
Man woman child encircling
The purpose of each progression of hours

Why are we here? A question
Unfathomable because the reasons keep changing
And we, stumbling the road
Feel for miscellaneous vegetation
To strengthen our stand

And after we greet the yellow king star
We salute ourselves, revel
In our existence, marvel at our nakedness
Possessed in independant power
Challenge the king sun itself
Side by side to see which light shines brighter
Together plotting the renovation of this world
The evolution of harmonic revolution
Octaves as great as galaxies

Today I will create a small dent
Which the atmosphere will hardly notice
If I could just, If I could just not
Contribute to the mess
If I could this day build a great mansion
Seeded from pyramids
And the ancient accumulated abundance
Offer the challenge
How great can communities
Rise and revive what is true

When will knowledge cease to be child?
Mature to realization, our great merging
Sustaining the captured morning throughout
The cycle of daynight

Not color, but texture
Not prisoner, yet participant

Now open our eyes and tell me how
We know it is possible to realize our dreams

Now open wider, imagine
The water is clear and the Sun
Is standing next to us.

Sandra María Esteves

Transference

Don't come to me with expectations
Of who you think I should be
From some past when
You were going through changes

I'm not your mother who didn't hold you all day long
Or kiss away the rough cuts when you fell
I'm not your sister who wouldn't play with you
Mashing up your favorite toys on purpose
I'm not the lady upstairs who keeps you up all night
Playing Lawrence Welk Muzac
And I'm not your girlfriend who left you flat
The one who promised forever never to go
For whom you would never love another
Or the one who used you for sex
And forgot your first name
I'm not the one who beat you
For ten dollars and dinner
Or ate up your cookies and milk
Or gave you the wrong kind of presents
I'm not the schoolgirl you followed for breakfast
Or the secretary you rapped to at lunch
Or the whore who tricked you in the evening
With a case of advanced herpes
I'm not your neighbor who hates you
'Cause you have more roaches than them
Or the landlord who steals your rent
And leaves you out in the cold
I'm not the meter maid who gave you $300 in parking tickets

Or the kid who plugged your tires just for fun
Or the psycho who smashed your front windshield
Or the truck that hit your rear bumper and ran
I'm not the traffic court judge who insists you're the liar
Or the junkie who popped your trunk lock
And tried to steal your spare tire
I didn't take your virginity with empty promise
Or con you with a job for sex
And I'm definitely not the one who ripped off your mind
And did not allow you to speak your own tongue
Or tried to turn you slave or dog
No, I'm not the bitch who denies you your true history
Or tries to hide the beauty of yourself
I am not the colonizer or the oppressor
Or the sum total of your problems, I am not the enemy
I am not the one who never called you
To invite you to coffee and dinner
Nor the friend who never gave you friendship
Or the lover who did not know how to love

So when you come to me, don't assume
That you know me so well as that
Don't come with preconceptions
Or expect me to fit the mold you have created
Because we fit no molds
We have no limitations
And when you do come, bring me your hopes
Describe for me your visions, your dreams
Bring me your support and your inspiration
Your guidance and your faith
Your belief in our possibilities
Bring me the best that you can

Give me the chance to be
Myself and create symphonies like
The pastel dawn or the empty canvass
Before the first stroke of color is released

Come in a dialogue of we
You and me reacting, responding
Being, something new
Discovering.

En el lugar que corresponde
Para Margarita

Rosario, nuestra hermana mayor, no decía:
"Cumplí mi deuda, mis deberes sociales,
seguí el obligado estreno de vestidos.
Lucí la más encantadora sonrisa
que nunca se adaptara a una cadena.
He permutado mi conciencia igualitaria
por una aprobación de manos del amigo,
del compañero, del colega que entiende mucho menos que yo"
(y cosas por el estilo que no recuerdo ahora).

Yo encuentro que filosofías de esa clase
conducen a tristes resultados, hermanita.
La libertad se llama rebeldía,
se llama ser extraña, ser sola y además estarlo;
se llama no llorar
cuando después de una brillante discusión académica,
en la que empleas todo el claro sentido
con que naciste,
la lógica irrefutable que aprendiste en la ciencia,
viene un hombre (con las mejores intenciones
de ser cortés) y te dice:
"qué linda que te ves
cuando hablas en público."

Y sabes
que no escuchó ni una palabra,
porque al fin son ideas de mujer
que no hay por qué tomar en serio;
porque sólo nos definen para el mundo,
hermanita,
dos pestañas oscuras,
una boca entreabierta con gracia
y unos pechos que desmienten (incluso hacen innecesaria)
toda capacidad intelectual.

Salutación: Ave
(de mal agüero para tantos)

Hola María,
Petra,
Isabel, Esperanza, Justina,
Elena, Clara:
faltas somos de gracia
y estamos solas como siempre
entre todas las mujeres,
entre todos los dolores sin fruto,
con los vientres cansados
de producir lo que se espera de nosotras.

No santas,
sino humanas hermanas,
María, Petra,
Isabel, Esperanza, Justina,
Elena, Clara,
madres de todos los nacidos:
es hora ya de que cerremos
la avalancha de pecadores
es estas sociedades sin igual.
Quien quiera proliferar miseria
que se busque otros cuerpos,
ahora y en la hora de nuestro triunfo.
Así sea.

Gloria

a la madre,
a la hija,
al espíritu de aquella hermana
que ha caído.

Gloria
a tantas mujeres ignoradas
como lo eran siempre en un principio,
como no lo serán de ahora en adelante
por el esfuerzo de unas manos
que nada tienen de divinas.
Gloria a ellas
por los siglos de los siglos,
hasta que el mundo
      y el paraíso
      y el infierno
reconozcan
que una trinidad de dictadores
(celestiales o terrenales)
no traerá justicia
ni paz
ni pan pacífico
a ningún ser humano de buena voluntad.

Ana Castillo

I Don't Want to Know

i don't want to know
it will be like this:
ex-husband anxious
to get back to his
young wife
menopause pulling at
my insides
parents old
and so wise
solemnly waiting
understanding without
a word
        and there
like a dormant garden
at the end
of a long tedious road
that led from Japan to here
lying very still
the corpse that was my son

Ana Castillo

Not Just Because My Husband Said

if i had no poems left
i would be classified *working class intelligentsia*
my husband said
having to resort to teaching or research
grow cobwebs between my ears
if i had no poems left

if i did not sing in the morning
or before i went to bed, i'd be as good as dead
my husband said
struck dumb with morose silence or apathy
my children would distrust me
if i did not sing in the morning

if i could not place on the table
fresh fruit, vegetables tender and green
we would soon grow ill and lean
my husband said
we'd grow weak and mean and useless to our neighbors
if i could not place fresh fruit on the table.

The Antihero

the antihero
always gets the woman
not in the end
an anticlimax instead
in the end
spits on her
stretched out body
a spasmodic carpet
yearning still
washes himself

doesn't know why
it is that way searching
not finding finding
not wanting wanting more
or nothing
in the end the key is
to leave her yearning lest
she discover that is all

Ten Dry Summers Ago

you could've planted Bermuda grass,
your neighbor to the right says.
But no, you didn't
   . . . and yes it's true, your life
   never depended upon it . . .

so now I have to landscape
this bare and godless ground
that keeps eroding
   into flyaway dust
      changing hands
        as easily as identity

have to dance, pivoting
—as a Chicano would say
              "en un daimito"—
    watering this wasteland

have to keep it moist
   until it grows
   until there's room enough
          to hold
    your god and mine

Angela de Hoyos

How To Eat Crow On a Cold Sunday Morning

you start on the wings
nibbling, apologetic-like
because, after all
    it was you who held the gun
and fired pointblank
the minute you saw the whites of their eyes
just like the army sergeant
      always instructed you.

—Damn it, this thing's
gonna make me sick!

—No it won't. Go on. Eat the
blasted thing (for practice)

because you'll be sicker later on
when your friends
start giving you
an iceberg for a shoulder.

. . . So the giblets are dry and tough.
But you can digest them.

It's the gall bladder
—that green bag of biliousness—
that wants to gag your throat
in righteous retribution
refuses to budge
won't go up or down, just
        sticks there

makes you wish that long ago
you'd learned how to eat
a pound of prudence
        instead.

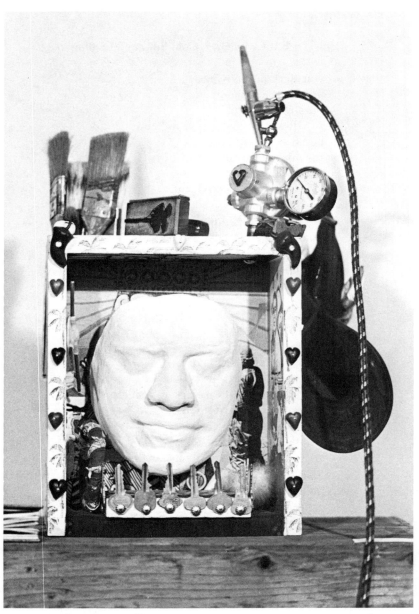

Portrait of Estevan Villa   *Patricia Rodríguez*

Judith Ortiz Cofer

Progress Report To a Dead Father

"Keep it simple, keep it short,"
you'd say to me, "Get to the point,"
when the hoard of words I had stored for you
like bits of bright tinsel in a squirrel's nest
distracted you from the simple "I love you"
that stayed at tongue-tip.

Father, I am no more succinct now than when
you were alive, the years have added reams
to my forever manuscript,
lists rile me now in your stead,
labeled "things to do today" and
"do not forget," lists of things
I will never do, lists that I write
remind me that I can never forget.

I can still hear you say,
"A place for everything and
everything in its place."
But chaos is my roommate now, Father,
and he entertains often.

Simplicity is for the strong-hearted,
you proved that through your brief
but thorough life, your days were stacked
like clean shirts in a drawer,
death was the point you drove home
the day your car met the wall,
your forehead split in two, not in your familiar frown,
but forever; a clean break.
"It was quick,"the doctor said, "He didn't feel a thing."

It was not your fault that love could not be
so easily put in its right place,
where I could find it when I needed it,
as the rest of your things, Father.

What The Gypsy Said To Her Children

We are like the dead
invisible to those who do not
want to see,
and color is our only protection against
the killing silence of their eyes,
the crimson of our tents pitched
like a scream
in the fields of our foes,
the amber warmth of our fires
where we gather to lift our voices
in the purple lament of our songs,
And beyond the scope of their senses
where all colors blend into one
we will build our cities of light,
we will carve them
out of the granite of their hatred,
with our own brown hands.

Achy Obejas

Kimberle

on the stone like white shadows indistinguishable
from the marble the heat the white shadows
the heat of young woman a woman white woman with
cavernous cheeks in a perfect face and the cheeks
are the flaw the error the pain the mistake imperfection
the cheeks with white shadows the stone and the
grain of the stone burning to the touch the white
heat of the stone indistinguishable

kimberle says no to the gods to the marble the
stones to the white heat that coarses her veins
the system the muscular arms that hang low with
no purpose (an exile) perfect face imperfect
face kimberle is friends with a spectre a black
coat hands that mechanically tease at her neck
at her sex at the holes in her cheeks the sick
yellow dog eyes that respond with enchanted disease
to the shadows and the heat from the stones that
burn to the touch start again start again kimberle

Sugarcane

can't cut
cut the cane
azuca' in chicago
dig it down to the
roots sprouting spray paint on the
walls on the hard cold
stone of the great gritty city
slums in chicago
with the mansions in the hole
in the head of
the old old rich left behind
from other times lopsided
gangster walls overgrown taken
over by the dark
and poor overgrown with no
sugarcane but you
can't can't cut
cut the water
bro'
from the flow and
you can't can't cut
cut the blood
lines from this island
train one by one throwing off
the chains siguaraya
no no
no se pue'e cortar
pan con ajo quisqueya
cuba y borinquen no
se pue'en parar

I saw it
saw black a-frica
down in the city
walking in chicago y
la cuba cuba
gritando en el solar
I saw it
saw quisqueya

brown
uptown in the city
cryin' in chicago
y borinquen
bro'
sin un
chavo igual but
you can't can't cut
cut the water
bro'
from the flow and
you can't can't cut
cut the blood
lines from this island
train one by one throwing off
the chains siguaraya
no no
no se pue'e cortar
pan con ajo quisqueya
cuba y borinquen no
se pue'en parar

¡azuca'!

The Bridge People

in the mornings you can see them
crawling out of their natural environs
yawning, stretching, slithering out of their foxholes
along the bayou
where they find refuge and protection
when the city lights go out and day begins to break
but right now they are rising
it's time to scrounge for empty beer cans
take in some sun
maybe quench that thirst that's constant

in the mornings you can see them
crawling out of the bayou
like grotesque marsh creatures, man-made
they adopt the camouflaging colors
of mud and slime and water stagnant green
their clothes are the color of crude
as in the oil that pollutes
the once clean and vibrant waters
of the Buffalo Bayou

they ascend and descend as they please
amid the busy urban streets they wander
at once isolated and intermingled
with the higher forms of life
"bridge people," downtowners call them
"transcients" on their way to nowhere
"the scum of the earth" they are
creatures that fell from grace with life

against the majestic futuristic buildings
and hustle and bustle of downtown Houston
the winos, the hobos and bums
and other down-trodden beings
are stark reminders
of human vulnerability
and of time that must advance and waits on no one:
surely along the way
the weak, the susceptible, the damned
must meet their fate

for as spectacular as man's accomplishments have been
in this age of boundless future
wherein the limits of the intellect remain a mystery
that continues tugging at the soul for more
modern man has not yet succeeded
in altering that basic constitution
of the human animal

the society that we create
is like a laboratory zoo worthy of continued scientific study
here, creatures of all sorts co-exist:
precarious is the balance.

Evangelina Vigil

Dumb Broad!

dumb broad!
I'm believing it as I'm seeing it!
dumb broad!
keep your eyes on the road, stupid!
a passenger sits next to her
motionless
oblivious
or just doesn't care
why don't you comb your hair at home, you stupid broad!
hey!
I mean, I've seen women yank off their steam rollers at stop lights
brandish brush
and then drive, one-handed
while expertly arranging their hair
with a few quick precision strokes—
I've done it myself
you have to in order to get to work on time
but, oh! this is too much!
I cannot believe this!
look! now she's teasing her hair!
both of her hands are off the steering wheel!
stupid broad!
you'd better keep your eyes on the road!
I'd hate to be in the car in front of her

she can't see the traffic behind her
for she's got the rearview mirror in a perpendicular position
while she fixes her eye makeup
at first with quick casual glances
but now very intently
peering into hazard
I mean, I know one gets distracted sometimes
you know, you look into the mirror to fix your lipstick
and you end up re-doing your eyeshadow!
god! you know you should've worn hyacinth instead of celery!
it looks so different in the daylight!

look at her!
I can't believe she's teasing her hair!
and with both hands off the steering wheel
now I can't get over that!
and in fast moving bumper-to-bumper 8 a.m. traffic
at a five-point intersection
and at a school zone at that!
now you tell me if this is not a dumb broad!

my god!
and the passive passenger sits!
doesn't nudge!
involuntary purposeless conjecturing:
he's probably her husband who has simply given up on her
his bitching was of no use
or rather, he's probably one of those passive husbands
who doesn't give a shit
but then, maybe he's a carpooler with no choice in the matter
or simply unaware that his life is in danger

now wait a minute!
hey! I'm believing this as I'm seeing it!
she is now spraying her hair generously
in round swooping motions
utilizing both the rearview and sideview mirrors
which she has expertly adjusted
the traffic is of no concern to her
and the passenger remains a mannequin
except for one slow motion glance over and back
as she squirts the spray
on her mass of teased hair and his bald head

it's now four blocks later
there she drives ahead of me
sporting a splendid hair-do
she brakes on and off sporadically
as she shifts her weight around in her seat
finding a position of comfort
while tuning the radio
and flicking her bic at a cigarette that's stuck in her mouth
then she looks over
and puffs smoke into the face of her motionless passenger
who, obeyingly, hands her a cup of steaming coffee

dumb broad!

Evangelina Vigil

Telephone Line

there are two lines of post-noontime customers
waiting to pick up phones
they are displeased because:
it is storming outside
their umbrellas and legs and shoes are drenched
this damn line is gonna make them late back to work
and, worse, it doesn't seem to be going anywhere!

a young Black girl waits on customers at one counter
she is very very slow
at the other counter is another line of waiting customers
and no one waits on them
but the sign says "Form two lines here"
and they oblige

at the head of the line
stand a pair of Mexicanos
they're short of stature
with a boyish innocence about them
they're here like the rest of us
to pick up a telephone
for, as a voice informed me through the wires
"Ma Bell don't delive' no mo'"

"What color, style of phone and length of chord would you like?"
the girl asks mechanically
looking off into the distance
as if to find the answer there
you can tell she asks this question countless times a day
"¿Qué?" they respond simultaneously
from my perspective at the end of the line
their short-haired heads and skinny necks
look like two human question marks looking at each other
"What color do you want, blue . . . white . . . yellow . . . white?"
the girl repeats disinterestedly
they begin to comprehend as she points to the different color phones
repeating the question and rolling her eyes
they pause in thoughtful consideration
exchanging opinions in Spanish
while assorted pairs of legs shift their weight impatiently

from right foot to left foot
from left foot to right foot
and perturbed expressions
and a side step over to the left to check and see
what's taking so damn long!
and a side step over back in line
and frustration and impatient sighs
and feet tapping to the tick of clocks
tip tap-tap-tap-tap tip tap-tap-tap-tap
that refuse to wait on unexpected delays
while the two Mexicanos make up their mind several times
as to what style, what color of phone, what length of chord they want

¡ah, qué vida en los Estados Unidos!
¡tierra de pura ventaja!
no more waiting in line at the Stop-n-Go phone booths
no more quarters lost
no more standing for hours at the Seven-Eleven pay phones
waiting for that call from San Francisco del Rincón:
"¡ah, qué la Juana!
me prometió que me llamaba a las meras tres, ¡hombre!
¡Ya son después de las sies!
Bueno, pues . . . vámonos ya. ¡Ni modo!"

most likely they live in a multi-unit apartment building
along with a number of other undocumented residents
most likely the style and color of phone
little matters to the habitat's decor
although important is
the length of chord

wearing smiles of satisfaction on their faces
they walk off into the storm with no unbrellas
but phone, chord and directories held securely under their arms:
yes, indeed!
why, if they all pitch in for the monthly bill
it's all very worth it!
what a bargain from Ma Bell!
"Sí, costea! Sí, costea!"

Southern Boulevard

I wait at a candy store
near the El after school.
It is 1952, 53.

My father is walking
towards me,
he is walking through the minds
of men curled to the ground in dice,
he is smiling into snake-eyes and craps
without a single complaint.
He is without the losses of most men
who gamble to be faithful to their wives.

I nod. He nods
and buys me a Hershey bar
before we step into the back room
where there is a fat man and a phone
and cases of bottles and boxes of things
unimportant to me.
My father asks me to pick a winner
and I close my eyes and point down
to the horse racing sheet.
Este, este, I say.
Two dollars on Queen Yvonne, my father says.
Sapia, two dollars, the fat man says,
as he plucks a pencil from behind his ear
and scribbles a note.

My father and I walk out to the street
where the títeres are still shooting
the dice against the stoop.
Oye viejo, they call, ¿tienes un peso?
My father ignores them
and hand in hand we pass
taking our chances with us.

Yvonne Sapia

The Landlord's Dream Of Hell

Collecting coins from the dead,
you fawn through dark halls
pissed in by night-tramps and satyrs.
The steps stick to your shoes.

The new tenant cooks chorizo in #2.
The blind man weeps with intensity in #5.
The widow in #6 repeatedly tests her mortality.
And #8 has not paid.
No stroke of luck here.
Even the door looks impoverished.
You knock on its indigent face
and threaten the missing with recognition.
A woman speaks through the door.
A child's voice translates
the mother's destitution into English,
warns of an elegant machete.

You slap the peeling paint
with demands and inconvenience.
She opens the slow door and wind lifts the shade,
sunlight striking her brittle hand.
A mirror at the entrance repeats you
as darkness laps helplessly behind.
And nothing stands in the way of the hardening knife.
The slight hand rests on your throat
with the culpable tool
of a woman irreversible in her desperation.

Del Medio Del Sueño

My mother's face blushing
above me like a lung
checks my eyes to be assured
I am trapped somewhere
in the walls of my dream.
She glides in quietness to my dresser,
shifts the intimate fabrics around
like fresh evidence.
Del medio del sueño,
I am not so far that I cannot come back
to watch her wear down in purpose.

She thinks I hate her food.
She thinks I listen at the bathroom door
when she washes what the doctors cut.
Sometimes she forgets who I am,
asks for the keys to the house.
Sometimes she forgets who she is,
asks to be walked to the ocean.

My father yearns to be patient,
then bites his fingernails
and sorrowfully turns to the television.
I pretend to go to sleep
and wait in the insomnia dark
for my mother and her suspicions
to verify the passing of nights
which permit few easy exits.

The Posture Of The Dance

My mother
is dancing.

First in the kitchen.
Then in the livingroom.

She is dancing to the scratchy
songs of her childhood,
rousing a sense of place.

She glistens with
recent invigoration.

Her music is loud.
Her housedress is loud.

But the passage of time
is the most intrusive sound.

For her legs do not speak
nor hear the miseries
of the long road to truth.

Her legs shape the dance
and ask for god's love.

That she can see the world
and continue to dance
is the miracle of life.

Pat Mora

Bailando

I will remember you dancing,
spinning round and round
a young girl in Mexico,
your long, black hair free in the wind,
spinning round and round
a young woman at village dances
your long, blue dress swaying
to the beat of *La Varsoviana*,
smiling into the eyes of your partners,
years later smiling into your eyes
when I'd reach up to dance with you,
my dear aunt, who years later
danced with my children,
you, white-haired but still young
waltzing on your ninetieth birthday,
more beautiful than the orchid
pinned on your shoulder,
tottering now when you walk
but saying to me, *"Estoy bailando,"*
and laughing.

Elena

My Spanish isn't enough.
I remember how I'd smile
listening to my little ones,
understanding every word they'd say,
their jokes, their songs, their plots.
    Vamos a pedirle dulces a mamá. Vamos.
But that was in Mexico.
Now my children go to American high schools.
They speak English. At night they sit around
the kitchen table, laugh with one another.
I stand by the stove and feel dumb, alone.
I bought a book to learn English.
My husband frowned, drank more beer.
My oldest said, "*Mamá*, he doesn't want you
to be smarter than he is." I'm forty,
embarrassed at mispronouncing words,
embarrassed at the laughter of my children,
the grocer, the mailman. Sometimes I take
my English book and lock myself in the bathroom,
say the thick words softly,
for if I stop trying, I will be deaf
when my children need my help.

Tía Ester
(a song of remembrance)

Tía Ester. Aunt Esther.
The words conjure up a dear image.
Round, rosy cheeks; clear, brown eyes.
Dimples. Especially dimples.
Even her fine,
        expressive
           hands
              were dimpled.
Long, long hair, oft times braided, coiled,
With beaded combs to hold it tight.

I beaded her combs when I was a teen
Forming her name—or flowers—
In pink, her favorite color.

From earliest childhood, my memories,
And those of her other children—
        (she gave birth to none—
But any child who appears at her door,
Qualified by simplest need—Is hers)
My memories of her recollect:
Her oatmeal . . . thin and lumpy, sweet and chocolate-y,
We ate it because she had made it.

But there was better. Her beans, tortillas,
        enchiladas, picadillo,
          fresh figs,
             watermelons under the trees
For she fed us always. She stuffed us.
And she loved us. With each morsel of food,
She instilled in us a deep love
of goodness, of kindness, of innocence.
Food and love were intermingled
Forever
In Aunt Esther's house.

And she told us stories, Bible stories;
In a Thespian role, in her Sunday school,
        she dramatized

Eyes sparkling, dimples deepening,
Samson contra los Filisteos.
David y Goliath.
King David. King Solomon. Queen Esther.
Ruth and Noemí. Moses. Noah.
All lived and marched before us,
Never to be forgotten in her words.

And at home.
Cradled in her deep bosom—
Warm and safe next to the great, beating heart,
There was no outside world.
Only love and Jesus.
And the faint smell of Vicks and Campho-Phenique.

These were Aunt Esther's remedies for most
earthly ills
That feeding could not cure.
From ant bites to flu—to an ache in one's psyche,
Vick's on the chest; a cup of hot herb tea,
And love.
Always love.

She took care of all of us all of her life.
Parents, siblings, nieces and nephews,
Grand-nieces and grand-nephews.
The old, the sick, the pastor's wife's puppy,
Sometimes we scarcely noticed
That she, herself, was often ill.
Her smile remained. Her strength,
She regularly spent for others.
Once she had an 8-lb. cancerous tumor
In her womb.
I knew, and did not worry,
That God would heal her.
And he did.
The doctors called it
a miracle, and it was.
But God could not do otherwise:
We needed her so.

For twenty more years, smaller illnesses
Plagued her flesh. But she remained glad
And praised her Lord every day.

Some others wondered at her naiveté. They
Did not understand,
Simple spelling and purpose behind her wisdom,
Especially at the end. She suffered so . . .
But her wisdom was that named by our Lord,
"Except . . . ye become as little children . . ."
Aunt Esther, Beloved Tía Ester.
You have surely inherited,
The Kingdom of Heaven!

If God does.....to remind us of His great Love,
To bring Jesus and Christ-like love,
To life for us.......
Form once in a lifetime—of human clay—
An Aunt Esther. And He did.
Then God is good; God is Love;
And I want to go to Heaven.

Cordelia Candelaria

¿Sin Raíces Hay Flor?

No history
So she tried to buy one
paying dearly for fringed rugs
she hung like relic tapestries
next to the Queen Anne chairs from Sears.
She spoke of Mamá Grande y Tías Queridas
by the dozen and casually wore
shabby woolen shawls that moths had visited
at the Goodwill.

One unkind day her story broke upon her
suddenly—like an egg cracked sharply—
and out spilled the messy query
that left her wet with shiny tears—

Without a history

hay

Fresh Mint Garden

My folks planted the yerba buena yesterday
in the northwest corner of our yard where
the faucet's run-off will keep the spearmint
wet and unmetaphysical.
They tilled the moistness tidily, working the cowdung
neatly into the earth till the ground resembled
an old lace mantilla clumsily forgotten outdoors
in the corner where I stood wondering
why "yerba buena" rests nicer in the evening air
among the crowds of childhood me's bobbing in the shadows,
where ollas of pale green liquid pour into the bathwater
to soothe fresh scratches from walks in chamizo,
where sprigs of yerba buena swim greenly
in teapots of boiling water, fragrant haikus
in oceans of prose.
Cuando acabaron con el jardincito
they pulled each other up off their knees,
arranged a few stray leaves
and looked at me.

Isleta

This not being a year for local color
few from Canyon Road
will come to paint you.
Yet the sun and seasons rising
over the blue Manzanos
and the great river
brown like the earth
will summer banks with cottonwood and willow,
whiten Decembers with floating snow.
Your vineyards, orchards,
low abode dwellings
slope gently eastward to the Rio Grande.

In your center
in the kiva
the growing center of light
beckons the dancers
the dance begins.

Año 1540
Alvarado followed golden dreamers
camped beside your bend of river
and called it "el Río de Nuestra Señora."
You rose brown upon the islet-
Isleta
and he dreamed of
the white twin crossed church
his coming would bring you.

At the northern outskirts,
off the road to Albuquerque
behind the white stucco house,
the red haired woman
bends to bake round loaves
in the round earth oven.
Each of her twelve children
was baptized in San Agustín
on the north side of the plaza.
In the central kiva
each was given a sacred name

that she will never know,
she is not Tanoan
and does not speak Tiwa.
Not even the padre speaks Tiwa.
He refuses a name for baptism
unless it can follow María, José or Juan.

Años 1620 a 1629
The Humanos Indians
have seen visions in their distant pueblo
of the lovely lady dressed
in flowing garments
who speaks to them in their tongue
of the holy church.
Each summer they send
a party of men west
over the plains and the Rio Grande
to the padres at Isleta.
Favor de venir a nuestro pueblo
a bautizar a la gente.
But the padres cannot.
They are too few in the river kingdom.
In Spain
Mother María de Jesús of Agreda
tells of visions,
of angels who transport her to New Mexico
to be with the Humanos people.
Word is sent to Mexico
then messengers to Isleta.
The padres hurry eastward
across the river and plains.

Año 1619
In order to preserve the culture
a command of Governor Eulate
permits the people their ancient dances.
Angered, Fray Salvador dons upon his head
a crown of thorns
and moves amongst the dancing
islet people
a heavy wooden cross across his shoulders.

Remember the Christmas eve
the Monsignor nailed the front pews

to the floor so the people couldn't dance?
Rafaela has come from Albuquerque
for her first midnight mass.
The wooden altar saints appear
to dance before her drowsy eyes.
To stop the dancing
she closes her eyes
reopens them to santos
swaying to candle flames.

Weary of early morning buses
north from the pueblo,
Terry studies nursing at St. Vincents
and works the soda fountain at Gishes
scooping cones for South Valley children
clutching nickels in dusty hands.
Her studies done,
she will find rooms in the city

Año 1691
It is the season
when yellow leaves the trees
and Vargas finds only church walls
standing in early snow.
Many have gone to Mexico
where they will find Isleta del Sur.
Others are west with the Hopi
but will return when there is calm
between the Spanish and river people.

No summer classes at Los Lunas High
So Carlotta travels daily
to Albuquerque to study algebra.
She has invited her classmate to Isleta.
Outside the doorway of the small adobe house,
Ana watches Carlotta's brother scatter
corn to the chickens. From within,
the softness of Tiwa-Carlotta
then her grandmother.
On the bus back
Ana remembers the flattened
tin can patches
on the brown adobe wall.
Mi abuela piensa que eres gringa.

In the front seats the tourists compare
postcards and turquoise rings.
Ana watches Isleta become smaller
whole and disappear
to be transported
to Boston in color photos
to Newark in bracelets and beads.

      In the kiva
      the ritual dust has settled
      and will settle again.
      The setting sun reddens the sky.
      On ancient flat rooftops
      red chile dries
      beside blue and yellow maize.
      Shadows of children fish ditches
      beside silent fathers.

Naomi Lockwood Barletta

En el Norte

La indiferencia de los edificios
me hace callar la rabia
que es la cordillera de mi ser.
Yo nací del verde
cubierta de lo vegetal.
Mis palabras aquí se mueren
como muere mi pueblo
sílaba por sílaba
hasta llegar a ser silencio
y nada más.

Naomi Lockwood Barletta

El Salvador

Si la lluvia
se confunde con la sangre
en una tierra de plomo,
si las madres ya no lloran
mirando el aire
que ocupa el lugar
de hijo tras hijo,
si los versos dejan
sus palabras de amor lujoso
es porque la muerte sonríe
con boca abierta:
hambrientos los sonidos,
satisfecho el silencio.

Marjorie Agosin

La mesa de Billar en New Bedford, Mass.

Ella entró vestida
era clara y encorvada como un día cualquiera
o como un otro día,
ella era redonda y joven
con algo de Eva y con algo de María.
Pero, ellos la vieron desnuda,
entraron bruscos por su pelo largo,
su pelo como cenizas
ellos la habitaban por las rendijas de sus ojos que se
    nublaban
mientras los falos asustados
la despedazaban como un trapo malgastado entre las
    cacerolas.

Ella entró vestida
como una luna
y le fueron deshojando sus misterios
sus faldas que se mecían
entre los dientes de los enanos rompiéndole, escupiéndola,
    acariciándola,
vagamente, torpemente.

Ella era celeste y vestía colores de río,
y ahora coagulada, fermentada, deforme
en una mesa de billar
New Bedford, Mass
pueblo de ballenas y hombres malolientes.

En la mesa de billar
ella flotaba eternamente abierta despojada de claridades
y ellos urgeteaban su vagina que ahora humeaba como una
    cloaca
como una boca de ballena náufraga
incendiada entre los despojos.

Su blusa
era una ráfaga de humos chamusqueada
y ellos no la veían
ya no la veían desnuda
porque era una enrollada presa de colores púrpuros en

una mesa de billar
sus brazos inutilizados
no podrían colgarse del que tal vez le quiso
y ahora como una carne en una carnicería de velorios,
    amarrada a la mesa de billar

Ella duerme desnuda.

Marjorie Agosin

Estados Unidos

Estados Unidos,
yo no invoco tu nombre
en vano,
ni te acuso por
desvirginar tantas estrellas
solo me adhiero
a tus inmensas soledades
y entiendo que no es tu culpa
el haber inventado la vida en
ready-made
ni los anocheceres dorados
de Miss Monroe,
Aunque confiésate
que gozabas de la triste enfermedad
de los pueblos mansos
y trepaste hasta la vía andina
para llenarte de cobres, cromosomas, de fusil
pero pensándolo bien.
Me paseo por Managua, El Salvador
por la Avenida Providencia en Santiago de Chile
y todos vestimos botas de Cowboy
en un sordo diálogo de Rock and Roll.

Mis pies

Hoy he vuelto
a detenerme
en mis pies,
son estrechos
como una niña
de la
China,
o una mujer que nunca
pudo ser princesa,
mis pies
son dos enanos benignos
que me sujetan
mientres hago memoria
de parajes y océanos.

Mis pies son arqueados
como una espalda que desde
lejos nos besa,
tienen cinco dedos que los he llegado
a nombrar
de tanto quererlos,
de tanto guarecerlos
del sopor de la lluvia
o del sol
enlazado
con el agua
que los baña.

Hoy refrigero mis pies
en una poza de agua bendita
donde tantos otros
han vuelto
para pedir
favores, recuerdos,
o para poder caminar
otra vez sobre la tierra
y yo los miro,
son dos alas
que han anclado
los viajes

junto a mí
o dos faros acompañándome

Y hoy están conmigo,
los pellizco mientras les escribo
estos versos
parecen ser de verdad
como mi memoria que
los sostiene
o como un camino
que van abriendo
por las ramas.

¿Dónde Están?

Los desaparecidos,
¿dónde estan?
¿Donde está el Miguel con el pan en los bolsillos?
¿Donde está la señora Rosa?
y el eco de la sangre
empaña preguntas,
y el aire se me mancha como la sangre.

Una rajadura,
una costra como un grito en el sepulcro,
vaticinan que las gargantas segregan silencios,
palabras nunca y siempre dichas
despedidas del amanecer y el amor.

Yo soy hembra sin fusil
pequeña y de cabellos azules como el ácido
que busca tras los hospitales de una morgue improvisada
tras iglesias censuradas
tras los signos de mis viudas
entonces
yo juro apoderarme de la palabra
ir con ella por los muros de la cuidad
ir con ella donde anduvo el látigo
ir con esta palabra
que Dios no me dio
al encuentro de las bocas desdentadas
como el hambre
ir en busca de tus ojos.

Yo juro ser la palabra
pero nunca lamentar a los
muertos que hoy y siempre
están.

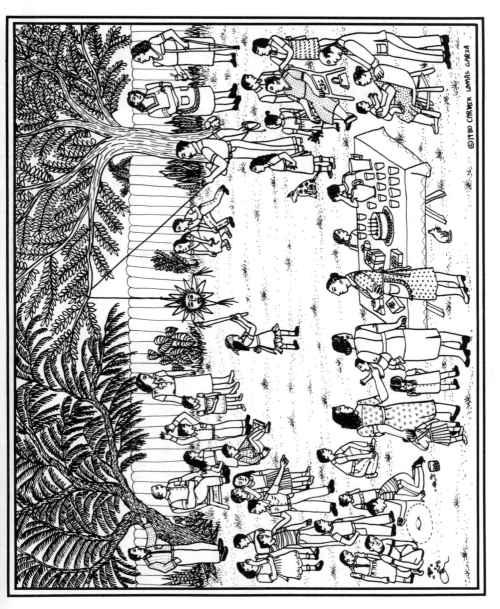

Cumpleaños   *Carmen Lomas Garza*

77

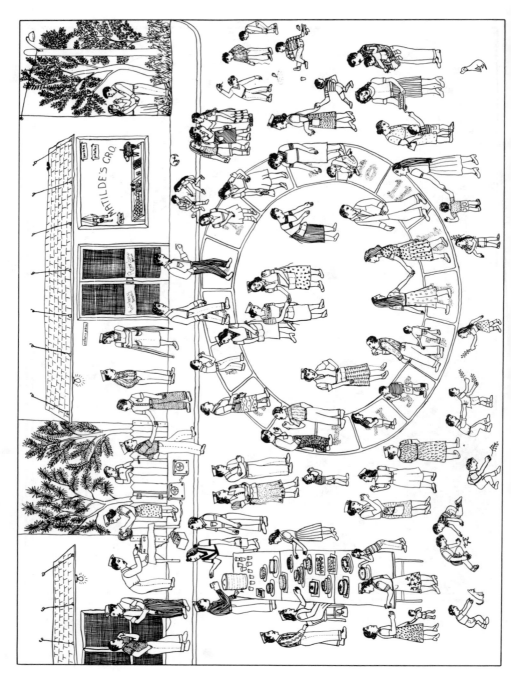

Cakewalk

Carmen Lomas Garza

Curandera   *Carmen Lomas Garza*

Nopalitos Frescos   *Carmen Lomas Garza*

Nopalitos   *Carmen Lomas Garza*

Silviana Wood

Dreams By Appointment Only

Irene Mendoza was connecting the green plastic water hose to the hot water faucet in the kitchen sink when she heard a car stop in front of her house. Immediately she felt afraid. She breathed deeply, walked to the living room, pinched the red and purple flowered curtain with her thumb and index finger, and stood sideways to see who it was without being seen herself. It was Miss Diodado, her Social Worker, arriving for the required Unscheduled Home Visit.

Irene dropped her hand, looked around the clean, neat living room, walked to the center table, and moved the bouquet of yellow and orange chrysanthemums closer to the middle. The spider 'mums' were plastic. She opened the door. The game began: Irene Mendoza and Lorraine Diodado played their roles with speeded animation.

"Hi, Irene. How are you? May I come in? Thank you. And how are the kids? Wonderful. My, my. How do you keep your place so clean? And with four kids?" Miss Diodado never stopped to listen to responses; she quickly checked off the appropriate boxes on the forms held in her clipboard.

"Three. Three kids." Irene corrected her on cue as she led the Social Worker to the sofa.

"Three?" Miss Diodado was smiling as she sat down, moving the chrysanthemums to the side to make room for her Monthly Progress Reports. Irene pushed the bouquet to the center again.

Miss Diodado was unlike the other Social Workers Irene had been assigned the past nine years. She was a young Italian from New York and living in Tucson had transformed her.

She wore long braids tied with leather thongs, hand embroidered peasant blouses from Guatemala, unhemmed, patched denim skirts, and Mexican *guaraches* on her feet; and she never shaved her underarms or legs, or wore any make-up now, but she looked very pretty with her sunburnt and peeling small nose, her thickly-lashed eyes with aquamarine contact lenses, and her very friendly smile with its perfect set of straightened teeth.

"Now then. This shouldn't take long. We just need an updated Status Report." She was playing the role that reminded Irene of Miss McIlhenny, her first Social Worker; she wrinkled her nose and pursed her lips. "Let's see. Mariana, oldest daughter, age seventeen, in high school, right? Jose, junior, sixteen, high school, right? and Susana, age nine, fourth grade, right?" She checked her digital watch. "Finished."

"Aren't you going to check the house for Unreported Residents?" Irene prompted her.

"Aha. Wait 'til you hear this." Miss Diodado pretended to be a television news announcer, holding an imaginary microphone to her mouth. "In San Jose, California, welfare officials, in an unprecedented night sweep, rounded up over twenty Unreported Residents, including, get this, an unidentified male who was plucking feathers off a chicken."

"So, step into my bathroom, I might have someone taking an Avon bubble bath." Irene led a groaning Miss Diodado to the bathroom between the two bedrooms.

"Are those your tennis shoes?" Miss Diodado pointed to the size eleven shoes on top of the dirty clothes in the laundry basket.

"No, they're Jose's. He left them for me to wash today." Irene picked up the gym shoes and held them close to Miss Diodado's nose. Miss Diodado squinted at the name stencilled near the rubber sole, pushed them away, and walked through the second bedroom, the kitchen, and back to the living room.

"That's it for the Unscheduled Home Visit." She found another form and frowned. "Oh, damn, I forgot this one. How old are you?"

"Thirty four."

"Good. The cut-off age is forty."

"Forty? What are you talking about?" Irene was confused with these new lines. "I thought I would get welfare until Susana's eighteen. By then I'll be forty-three, I think, and probably working—"

"Wait a second, Irene. You can keep getting welfare as long as you have minor children in school. The cut-off age that I'm talking about is for the new grant: Special Instruction and Training. If you pass the tests they'll send you to training for nine months at the community college. This way they figure you'll be trained and ready to work by the time Mariana and Jose finish high school. And it would probably be just a part-time job since Susana would still be coming home early. Now, here's your appointment card for next Thursday, and you'd better take a lunch with you 'cause it involves about six hours of testing."

"Testing? But I haven't been to school in—seventeen years."

"Not to worry. It's mostly speed, nuts and bolts stuff with your hands. Just go in and tell them you're there to take the tests for the Special Program for Instruction and Training. It's there on the card, see? I'd give you a ride but they're sending me to Phoenix."

"Phoenix?" Irene felt as though she was echoing.

"Just for a week; I'll be back, don't worry."

Irene didn't understand but she was silent. Miss Diodado stood waiting, expectantly. Irene walked to the record player next to the chair across from the sofa. She opened the case: Miss Diodado kicked off her *guaraches*. Irene cleaned the needle. Miss Diodado moved around the center table. Irene pushed the button and placed the needle on the record already there. The record played.

"*Cumbia!*" Miss Diodado was dancing, spinning. "Step, step together, step. C'mon, Irene, teach me to pivot before I hit the wall."

"You've got it, Lorrie. Pivot with your left foot. That's it. Perfect. Come dance into the kitchen for some coffee."

"But what about my hands?"

"Pretend you're playing *maracas*. And move your shoulders. That's it. You've finally got it."

They drank coffee and ate refried bean burritos.

"Lorraine, were you serious about that college thing?"

"Yeah, I had to make the appointment for you. My supervisor went through my files."

"Lorrie, I'm scared. And don't give me that 'not to worry' line of yours."

"I won't, I won't. Listen, Irene, take the damn tests first and we'll take it from there."

"Is it a lot of reading? English stuff, I mean."

"I really don't know. Like I said, it's mostly speed, with the hands, putting round pegs into square holes. Maybe some spelling. What the hell do I know? So you flunk the tests, what can they do to you? Listen, I have to run now. Thanks for my *cumbia* lesson. Let's just hope my date knows how to dance, right?"

"It's nothing." Irene walked her to the door. "But I swear, Lorriane Diodado, the next time you ask me whose tennis shoes those are, I'm gonna shove them—"

Lorraine left and Irene finished the laundry. She kept thinking of her high school days and tried to picture herself in school again. She remembered the wild times mostly: the rides to the cemetery at the west end of town where she and Jose necked among the graves; drinking White Port wine with lemon juice before going to the *tardeadas*— dances that started at four in the afternoon and ended at four in the morning, at the Casino, Amvets, or La Victoria ballrooms; dragging South Sixth in Jose's Chevy after the *chubascos,* splashing water into the other cars, and ending up at a drive-in restaurant for fish and chips or chile dogs and French fries; and finally, running away to Nogales when she was seventeen to get married.

The marriage had lasted eight years, four months.

It bothered her that she couldn't remember school events so she forced mental images of chalk, blackboards, books, paper, and the sweet white glue she loved to eat. She couldn't remember ever learning anything, and the thought of the welfare tests scared her. Well, she reassured herself, she had learned to read. Finally. From kindergarten and up to the third grade she had sat and turned pages when everyone else turned his, never understanding the printed words, never understanding the teacher who spoke only English. At the end of the school year everyone had been promoted to the fourth grade but she'd had to repeat the third grade. Again.

That summer, before school started, she played hopscotch with the Garcia kids. She was winning with her lucky piece of chain when the Garcia's were called in to supper before the game ended. So Irene sat alone, writing letters with her finger on the soft dirt. Somehow the letters began to connect and turn into words. Puff. See Puff run. Dick and Jane. See Dick and Jane play with Puff and Spot!!!

From that day on she read everything: the government-issued surplus oatmeal boxes and cans of milk on the table, the stolen comic books from the Chinaman's grocery store, and the Methodist Bible she got when she switched religions for one day to get it.

She found the library downtown, and it was far enough that she could walk, check out three books, and finish reading them by the time she reached her home. Back in school she would now read faster than anyone else; she would hold her finger to the page the rest were reading, and she would read on to the end. If she wasn't asked to read aloud, she would draw flowers on the desktop with her pencil, erasing them with saliva, or daydream as she stared out the window.

The reading never lost its magic until she went to high school, met Jose, started ditching classes for the wild times with him, and now all that she could remember were the mandatory book reports she'd had to write: someone rolling two steel balls in his hands as she went crazy; someone stealing bread and living in the sewer with rats; a woman knitting names into a scarf as heads got chopped off; and Huck Finn loving a black slave named Jim. She had finally quit school when she was seventeen.

And now college. Vocational college. Seventeen years later.

Irene drained the rinse water into the Chinaberry tree and went inside to cook dinner.

That night, when they were all watching television, she told her children she might be going to school.

"You're too old," Mariana said.

"For how long?" Jose asked.

"I'm not sure, maybe for two semesters. Nine months."

"Nine months! That's forever," said Susana, as she bounced up and down on the sofa.

Susana's jumping made the television picture turn sideways, and Jose went to straighten the bent clothes hanger that served as the antenna—sometimes bent, sometimes straight.

The next day Irene went to visit her mother. She would do her mother's housework while her mother talked on and on without stopping.

"Here, have some coffee, I just made it; I know you won't drink it if it's reheated, *tan fastidiosa*, sit down, never mind those dishes, they can wait, I never get to see you. *Siempre metida en tu casa,* you never find time to visit your own mother; put some milk in your coffee, you're too skinny."

Irene drank her black coffee.

"Which reminds me, Irene, where did you leave my dream book the last time you cleaned out my cupboards? You know I need it; I use it every day. Yesterday, poor Mrs. Gallardo, you know her, her husband died just six months ago, or was it longer? Before he died she had dreamed a wedding, and you know that means death for sure; I didn't have the heart to tell her, her husband already looked moribund, it was a bad sign when he got all that money from the court after the accident. Anyway, to get to the point, she came over because she'd had a dream of a rifle and I couldn't find my book. So I told her it meant she'd come into some money."

"Money? I thought you said dreaming a rifle meant sex."

"Same thing. I hope she does come into some money, though. She owes me five dollars since last month, or was it two months? So where's my book?"

"In your dresser. First drawer."

"What a memory. You got that from me, you know. It's funny, I'm the one who's always telling people their dreams, and now I have to see what my own dream means."

"So what did you dream?" Irene asked after her mother found the dream book; she didn't believe in dream interpretation but she liked to humour her mother.

"Strange dream. I was drinking water from a dipper. You know the kind, like a gourd shell. Those gourd shells really keep the water cool. Back in the ranch in Mexico, we used to keep one next to the well, but then of course the water from the well was already very cold. Did I tell you the joke about the toothless old woman who offered the stranger water with her gourd and he drank from the side of the handle because he felt repulsed by her, and she tells him that's *her* favorite side for drinking water?" She laughed.

"Doesn't water have a lot of meanings?"

"Never mind the water." Her mother thumbed the worn pages. "Here it is: Dipper: drinking from any kind of dipper is a warning to guard against the impulsive breach of family, no matter what the provocation, hold your tongue or you will regret it.' So what does that mean?" She handed Irene the book.

"Well, I hope that it means that whatever I say to you today, you won't be able to tell me anything about it."

"Nothing?"

"Nothing. Or you'll regret it." Irene liked this dream.

"Hmmph. That's the last time I dream dippers."

Irene got up from the table and finished washing the sink-full of dishes.

"Lorraine says there's a chance I may be going to college."

"College? A woman your age, with children, has no business going to college." Irene could tell that her mother remembered the dream's warning. "But my mouth is closed."

"I can't live on welfare forever."

"So get married again. I know lots of women who are getting married two times, even three times. It's the modern way. You had a good man; I don't like to talk bad of anybody, so he drank his beers and fooled around, what man doesn't?"

Irene walked to the bed and changed the sheets. Then she got the laundry basket and started to fold the clothes she had washed the week before. Her mother followed her whenever she moved.

"You said Jose left you because he didn't want any more kids and you got pregnant with Susana, but I think it was because of the way you are. You always wanted everything perfect, just like your father, may he rest in peace, even if he was a son-of-a-bitch, sometimes, like dying off when I was in my prime, not like Mrs. Gallardo, past sixty, but nothing's perfect. When you were a little girl you wouldn't eat the egg if I busted the yolk or overcooked it. So you tell me, who can fry a perfect egg?"

Irene got her purse and walked to the door.

"I have to leave, Mom. It's almost time for Susana to come out of school."

"Here, take the kids some sweet bread, it's not too hard; tell them to dunk it into the milk, like I do. And, Irene, my daughter, don't worry about the college thing. If worse comes to worse, I'll move in with you. To help you."

It was a new community college; the cement smelled wet still.

After she passed the welfare tests, Irene went to register for her classes. School had already been in session for about one month but the welfare trainees were allowed to register late. Irene wondered when the students actually went to classes; they seemed to be lazily lounging all over, reading, waiting for the bus, drinking cokes. Everywhere she looked she saw young girls in shorts and halter tops, wearing no brassieres underneath, and bare-chested boys flying Frisbees in the air, and many dogs chasing and barking around them. She had no idea where the Administration Building was but she felt too afraid, embarrassed to ask, so she walked very fast as though she knew where she was going.

She found the building and only one other person was in line for the vocational training grant. The girl there sent her to an advisor after telling her the required courses and their numbers. The advisor had to sign the forms. The door to his office was locked so Irene sat on the floor and smoked a cigarette while she waited for him.

"Waiting for me? Sorry I'm late. Come on in." He walked to his desk and unpacked his lunch. "Have a seat." He stared at her cigarette.

Irene sat down and faced his desk. He had two signs pasted on the front: "Today is the beginning of the rest of your life." and "Thank you for not smoking." She put out her cigarette on the lung-shaped ashtray and handed him the forms. She stared at him.

His hair was long and tied into a pony-tail with a rubberband; his cotton shirt had faded Spanish words advertising flour; his white pants were loose-fitting, like pajamas, and held at the waist with a many-colors woven belt, and he wore sandals made from automobile tires. He started to eat his sandwich as he signed the registration forms.

"Oh, oh." He stopped signing. "You left out English."

"What?" Irene was now staring at all his hanging plants.

"English. You need three units of English. You have the class schedule there, what's open for one o'clock?"

Irene nervously checked the schedule that was divided by subject, not hours.

"The girl said I just needed Typing, Shorthand, and Business Math." She handed him the schedule.

"She's wrong. That's just nine units; you need twelve units for the Special Instruction and Training grant." He bit into the whole wheat bread. "Let's see, Business English's at three."

"My little girl comes out of school at two. I have to be home for her. I can't stay here until four."

"Well, you really should take the Business English for that grant," he insisted as he read the class description to her, "'increases vocabulary and spelling skills.' But you did fine there. Let me call the supervisor." He dialed the welfare office. The bread was sticking to his front lower teeth and he pushed it off with his tongue.

Irene stood up and walked over to the nearest macrame planter that held a lush philodendron plant. She pinched off two yellowed leaves and stuck her finger in the planter to see if it needed water; it didn't.

The advisor took another bite; alfalfa sprouts hung from the corners of his mouth. He finished the telephone conversation and turned triumphantly to Irene.

"Just as I thought. You *do* need three units of English. Now here's the problem; we have an English class at one, Short Story, and Business English at three."

"I have to be home for my little girl—"

"Now let me finish." He picked his teeth with his little finger. "Mrs. Croesus, the supervisor, is willing to let you substitute the Short Story class this semester only. Next semester you *must* take the Business English or the welfare won't pay. So, since you have the babysitter problem at three, they'll accept the Short Story, all right?" He began to eat his sunflower seeds, raisins, and nuts.

"But what's that class? I don't like—"

"Nothing to it. Just reading short stories and discussions."

Irene was not satisfied but another student came to the door; the advisor burped gently and waved her off.

Even after a month on campus Irene felt like the old man who had fallen asleep under a tree for many years and had awakened to a strange new world. She felt out of place among the young students, the young teachers. She felt awkward, especially with the girls who seemed to range between two extremes: some looked as though they had just stepped out of the shower and into the classroom, with dripping wet hair, no make-up, cut-off Levi shorts, t-shirts with sexy slogans, barefooted or with rubber thongs on calloused feet; the others dressed like magazine fashion models, wearing gaucho skirts, boots, sweaters tied around their necks, turquoise rings on every finger, green eyeshadow, and glistening mocha-flavored lipstick.

And here she was: wearing her long brown hair pulled back, twisted into a bun, Mariana's rejected cherry red lipstick, bleached-stained shirts, her son's outgrown pants that were too short for her too, and her ankle bones stuck out from her tennis shoes. Would someone ask her, like Susana did, if she was expecting a flood? She was always alone, walking fast next to the cement walls, head down, books clutched to her chest.

Once, Lorraine surprised her as she walked out of the Typing class. At first Irene didn't recognize her; she had cut her hair, was wearing high heels and stockings, and was wearing a dress.

"Lorraine! What happened to you?"

"Cut my hair. Like it?" She put one hand on her hip, the other behind her neck and posed.

"Yes, I like it. But you're wearing a dress—"

"Listen, I hate it. But I got sick and tired of Personnel leaving me cute notes with copies of the Official Dress Code. If you can't beat them, join them, they say. But they'll never, never conquer my free spirit, right?"

"What brings you here, business? Or lunch?"

"Lunch. Well, business too. I had to drop off Progress Report forms."

"Progress Reports, here too? How about Unreported Residents?"

Both laughed as they walked down the steps to the cafeteria.

"Umm, *chimichangas*, my favorite. There goes my diet. One *chimichanga* with extra cheeze, please. Thanks." Lorraine ordered.

While eating, Irene told her about her classes.

"Typing was giving me problems. This little finger just couldn't hit the letter 'a' at first, but now I am really fast. And accurate. Shorthand's still like a foreign language but the squiggles are turning into words now.

My one headache is Business Math but Mariana helps me."

"What about Business English?"

"Didn't they tell you? I have the Short Story class instead."

"Wonderful. Did my supervisor, Medusa, approve it?"

"Just for this semester. I really like this class. It's my favorite. We just read the stories and discuss them. I love it. It's funny. When I read a short story now, it's like electricity, know what I mean?"

"No, I'm not much into reading."

"You know that feeling in the air before you get an electrical storm?"

"Well, my hair gets extra curly." Lorraine patted her head. "And I think I perspire more, is that what you mean?"

"Yeah, I guess I do. It's like my brain has two electrical wires and they connect—ZAP! But that's only when I really get the point of the story, sometimes I don't. What I haven't been able to figure out is *after* the storm, things are different. When I finish reading something seems to be missing—" Irene stopped.

Lorraine was trying to see what time it was.

"Am I boring you?"

"No, no. I'm sorry. Irene. It's just that I'm not that great on literature or art, or things like Shakespeare. I really have to run now; I've put in for a promotion and Medusa's watching every move I make so I can't be late. Don't worry about the stories, just enjoy them." She reached under the table. "My purse, my purse, my kingdom for my purse. See what I mean?"

Lorraine left and Irene set there alone until two boys came to sit at the table. They were making jokes about the cafeteria food, something about the "porcupine balls" they were eating. One joked about the "balls" and Irene looked up.

"Sorry, ma'am." But she hadn't understood the joke anyway so she said nothing and left.

At home she was always studying. Once she couldn't find her Business Math book and she saw it propped against the television hanger. She removed the book; the hanger fell and the picture rolled.

"Fuck," she said without thinking, after hearing the word at school all day.

"Mama said the 'F' word. Mama said the 'F' word," Susana shrieked happily, running to tell Mariana and Jose.

"Is that what they're teaching you in school?" Mariana aped her, one hand on her hip, pointing a finger with the other, just like Irene did.

Irene kept reading until she fell asleep on the couch and Jose woke her up.

"Mom. Hey, Mom, wake up. I gotta make my bed, Mom." He shook her gently by the shoulders.

She sat up. "The story about Gaston is about a man who buys his daughter two peaches. But one of the peaches had a worm; his name was Gaston—"

"You're dreaming, Mom."

Irene looked around, picked up her books, and went to bed with Susana who kicked all night. She dreamed of peaches and worms until the alarm rang. Maybe it was time to visit her mother; maybe dreams had meaning.

First of all, when she stepped inside, Irene was surprised to see that the floor was mopped and waxed, the sink was empty, the bed was made, with ruffled pillows on top, and her mother served her coffee in a matching cup and saucer.

"New dishes, Mother?"

"I just got them with the Green Stamps, three books. Put some milk in your coffee; you never pay attention to what I say. Do you remember Don Chico?"

"No."

"Yes, you do. Remember he came out in the paper when he was caught stealing from the church money for the poor people in Africa and the priest knocked out his teeth and said he would have shot him if he'd had a gun? Anyway, he was married to Vicenta Alvarez; she was a beauty, you'd never believe it to see her now, so fat, but that's from not taking care after having so many babies. They used to call her '*La Piernuda*' her legs were so pretty, before she got the varicose veins. She and her cousin, Carmela, used to fight like dogs over Don Chico when he was young and handsome, but of course neither one would want him now, toothless and useless. To make a long story short, she's moved back to this barrio, the snake."

"Vicenta's moved back?"

"No, pay attention. Carmela moved back. And that's not all. Do you know what she professes to be? A reader of cards, can you imagine? A charlatan, that's what she is. And I haven't told you the worst of it. Some of my very own clients are going to her. Secretly, but I know. Mrs. Gallardo let it slip out that Carmela's house is *so* clean, *vieja hipócrita*, never did pay me my money. How can anyone with intelligence believe that a card, a mere flip of the wrist, will make a difference in their lives? Now dreams, that's real, because dreams are your very own; I don't make them up, and I don't tell you what to dream, do I? If I did, I'd tell you to dream gardenias. But I don't. So, how's school?"

"I've been studying for the tests. And then I'll stay home for about a month, for Christmas vacation."

"Back in your cave. You know, at first I didn't like the idea of you going to school. But then I was glad you were getting out of the house. I don't understand. You never want to leave the house, visit friends, go dancing. That Social Worker is the only one you open the door to. I know, I know, don't ask me how I know. And you with so many friends, so popular. Even after Jose left you, after you had Susana you still were the same, so pretty, always smiling. And then you changed." Irene's mother sighed.

It was easier for Irene to tolerate her mother's endless chatter than her disappointed sighing, so Irene decided to end the visit. At the door she stopped.

"What did you mean, a while ago, that I should dream gardenias?"

"Gardenias? Ah, yes, gardenias. To dream gardenias means a new, passionate love affair. That's what you need to get you out of the house, and smiling again. Or, it can also mean that an old romance will flame again. Maybe Jose's coming back. Don't frown like that, you're gonna get a wrinkle right between your eyes. I'm gonna have to get you that face cream they have at Walgreen's, the one Sophia Loren uses. You don't see her with wrinkles, do you? Or is that the commerical for perfume? Well, I'll get you the cream *and* the perfume. Like the lady who pee'd in the ocean said: 'Every little bit helps.'"

Irene walked home slowly and thought of the lovers her mother never knew she'd had. It was after Jose had been gone over a year, the year when she had changed. At first, pregnant and alone, she'd cried, begging Jose's relatives to give her his address in California. They had been patient, polite, but then they'd hung up on her telephone calls, closed the door to her face, stopped talking to her. But her friends since childhood would visit her, give her rides to the clinic, invite her and her two older kids to parties, helped her. It all started after Susana's birth; Betty and Sam baptized her, and as moneyed godparents, they invited everyone to a grand bar-b-que. Irene was helping, peeling the green chile for the *salsa*, next to the fire, her cheeks red from the heat, when one of the husbands, pretending to check the briquets, stood close to her, whispered "You're looking good, *mamacita*," before the wife saw him, and called him back to her side. She'd then gone into the kitchen to wash the chile from her hands, two husbands were emptying bags of ice into the tin tub for the keg of beer. One asked her if the *salsa* would be hot, and she'd answered yes, very hot. The other husband teased her, saying only a jealous woman could make hot *salsa*, and that he liked a jealous woman. They laughed. On her way out, one of them, thinking she was already out the door, said something dirty, that she could peel *his* chile anytime! Feeling guilty, not knowing why or what she'd done, she busied herself for the rest of the celebration, serving plates, holding Susana or other babies so she wouldn't be asked to dance, cleaning, until finally Betty and Sam had taken her home.

She remembered this clearly but it was only the beginning. At other reunions the jokes continued, more brazen then suggestive, daring pats on her hips, or lower, obvious brushes against her breasts, horny husbands, jealous wives, accusations, denials, angry scenes. Then the lovers so that the husbands would leave her alone. Losers: Armando who wanted her to go with him to Phoenix, without Mariana, Josecito, and Susana; Ramon who worked at two jobs to send child support payments to two ex-wives; Alfonso who never worked but loved to sing, dance and write poetry.

It had all ended the night Susana was very sick; there was no lover, all the wives were at a baby shower, Irene wasn't invited, and she called Sam, her *compadre*, for a ride. Gee, he was sorry but he was babysitting, you know, Betty went to a shower, maybe Irene should call her there, did she want the number? No, he couldn't take her, he couldn't take his kids out, they had a cold, they were already asleep, why didn't she call?

Irene didn't know if that was the night she changed, when she'd stopped smiling, like her mother said, but the next day, when Susana had finally stopped vomiting, she'd had the phone disconnected, and she'd stopped opening the door. Anyway, not that many people had been knocking on her door.

Besides, Irene thought as she almost reached her house, she wasn't the only one; her neighbors were the same, they never talked to Irene either. The old woman on the right, the "witch," would always call the police on the kids playing baseball in the street, and she would never return their ball if it went into her yard. The young girl on the left would greet Irene only if they'd happen to meet going in or out of their house, even after the night the older boy had cut his feet on a broken bottle and had to be taken to Emergency for stitches and Irene had babysat their baby until close to three in the morning. Well, Irene thought, maybe everyone had a reason for closing the door to others.

It was like a game she'd invented with the Garcia kids, a combination of tag, freeze, and statues. No one knew who was "It." Lots were drawn, but if tagged with the secret signal you had to freeze into a statue. Eventually, if no one guessed who was "It," everyone would be a statue, except "It." Irene had been the best.

So let them all be statues; she had other things to worry about: studying, the final exams, the blue books she had to buy for the Short Story class. What the hell was a blue book anyway?

After two weeks, the teachers returned the finals, except the Short Story. Irene had gotten an "A" in all her other classes, and she waited impatiently for the last grade. She felt confident that she'd done well; she had read the two stories many times. The first story had been about the two sisters who were at a zoo, watching a blind bear who reminded them of a childhood friend. The second story had been about two Englishmen who were neighbors who met one morning and talked about the Japanese quince tree in the middle of their home. The last questions on the exam, the thematic statements and impact on characters and reader, gave Irene the most trouble. She'd had problems with these two stories when she'd first read them; they didn't seem to be saying anything. But Irene remembered the other students' discussion and tried to answer correctly: that the cruel and vicious treatment the sisters had received from their aunt had left them scarred and embittered towards life without their even realizing it; and that the two Englishmen felt very lonely, but their class structure, or something, prevented them from reaching out for the other's company or friendship.

Other students would ask the teacher when she'd finish grading their exam but she kept saying that the essay exams took longer. Irene kept leaving the class with a headache. Finally, the teacher was ready to hand them out. Before that, though, she gave a lecture on and on about her disappointment in some, her joy in others, the grade curve; and then she finally called the names. Each student walked up to the teacher who gave each a little talk as she handed each the blue book. Irene felt a steady throbbing pressure near her temples, and she rubbed them while she waited.

"Mendoza."

Irene felt weakness go through her body as she walked to the front of the class.

"Very good. I liked the details you gave. Shows you understood plot and conflict. All the elements, really, especially symbolism and characterization. Nice. Just a little problem with theme, I'd say."

Irene took the blue book and sat down, pleased, not hearing another word for ten minutes.

She opened the blue book; her eyes widened as she saw it all marked up with a red felt-tip pen. Abbreviations, arrows, lines, and unknown words seemed to jump from the pages. She turned to the last page: "Comp. B, Punct. and Grammar D, Grade C + ."

"Hey, what did you get?" the bearded Vietnam vet behind her asked.

"C + ."

"Bummer," he said, pushing his blue book into his fatigue green backpack.

Irene sat very still. Then she started to draw flowers in the margins that had no red markings. She turned the "C + " into a morning glory blossom with climbing vines. She turned to the window.

Fucking new college didn't even have fucking windows to stare out.

The welfare check for the month of July arrived along with a letter from Lorraine who had been transfered to Phoenix after her promotion to Supervisor. Irene placed the letter under the plastic chrysanthemums for later reading, and went to the grocery store to cash the check. Usually, she and the girls cleaned the house together, but today Mariana would do the housework and laundry alone to earn money for the carnival at the Southgate Shopping Center. She had even agreed to take Susana with her.

That night, alone, Irene read Lorraine's letter. She hated Phoenix, was thinking of moving to California where they paid more money, congratulated Irene for getting an "A" in every single class, except for the Short Story class, and "That didn't *really* count," and reassured Irene that with grades like that, she'd easily get assigned to a good job.

Irene reviewed her past school year. She could now type, take shorthand, give correct change, and spell and divide words properly. Business English had been exactly as the Advisor had said: "increases vocabulary and spelling skills." All she'd had to do was replace those troublesome electrical wires in her brain with a miniature camera that recorded, catalogued and filed without question, without nagging of needed action.

It was very hot; lightning flashed and thunder crashed, but it wouldn't rain. Still, Irene worried that the girls would be caught in the rainstorm, that they wouldn't find a ride home, that it was late and getting very dark, that Mariana for sure would lose Susana in the carnival crowd, that the electrical power would go out and the girls would be stuck high up on a dangerous ride, scared and helpless, that there would be a riot, a fire; Irene wanted to wake up Jose so that he could worry with her, too.

They walked in, laughing, describing the rides, the food, all the school friends they'd seen, the lightning and thunder that had made the rides even more exciting.

"You should've gone with us, Mom. It was fun. Mariana let me get on the "zipper," and the "Hammer," and the roller-coaster, and the "Fun House,"—that wasn't scary. And I got to eat cotton candy, corn-dog-on-a-stick, candy apple, popcorn, three cokes, and—I forgot what else," she was counting on her fingers.

Irene wiped the candied-apple syrup and cotton candy from Susana's cheeks, and struggled to get the instantly-sleepy Susana into her pajamas.

"Susanita, *marranita*," Irene teased her. "Little pig. You ate nothing but junk food. Tomorrow, I'm making a *caldo* with lots of meat and vegetables."

"Yuck!" She fell asleep.

"I bet she has nightmares, from the rides or from the junk she ate," she told Mariana.

"Nah, she won't; she's tough," Mariana answered.

And it was Irene who had the terrifying nightmare that sent her to her mother for an interpretation.

Right away Irene saw that her mothers' windows were cleaned and the curtains were stiffly-starched. On the front window, on the right hand corner, was taped a small sign: Dreams one o'clock to five o'clock

95

ONLY.

"Business is business," her mother explained. "I have lots of work to do. People can't just walk in and expect me to drop everything for their dreams, can they? No. And another thing, like the Bible says: 'You cannot serve two masters.' Or is that the income tax people? Anyway, they either come to see me, or they go to the charlatan with the cards. This is serious business, not like doctors or lawyers where you really need a second opinion, you know? So, what did you dream?"

"Oh, never mind. It was a stupid dream. I just got scared."

"Stupid? No dream is stupid. All dreams have meaning. You tell me the dream; I'll tell you if it was a stupid dream."

"I walked into a clown's mouth—"

"You walked into a clown's mouth?"

"Not a real clown. You know, the Fun House in a carnival, where the whole thing's built like a clown's head, and the door's his mouth. But that's not what I want you to look up."

"Well, clowns are easy. You just have to change friends."

"It's not the clown. I went inside, and there were trick mirrors and wind going up my skirt."

"Now I know what you mean. What else?"

"There was a spiral staircase and at the top, people would go down a slide and end up outside the Fun House. But when I started to climb the stairs, they folded under, and I kept holding on to the sides. The more I tried to climb, the more I could hear the clown laughing, like a record."

"Did you get to the top? That's important. Try to remember."

"I don't know."

Irene's mother wet her finger and turned the pages. "Aha. Here it is: 'Steps. See ladder.'" She found the page and read. She closed the book. "I never knew there was this much to ladders. It's good that you were going up, not down. If the steps break, which they did, folded under is the same as breaking, then you're not getting your greatest ambition, but you'll get financial security, which is even better. What's really bad luck is to have the ladder fall on top of you, or if you fall from the ladder, that's bad, too. Here, you read it."

"Never mind. I'll see you later. I'm cooking a *caldo*, and I left the meat boiling so I better go back."

"What about the welfare? When do they put you to work?"

"Soon. Lorraine says probably next week."

"Well, see? There's your financial security."

The chunks of beef were simmering slowly with garlic, onions, and one bay leaf. Irene washed the vegetables and spread them in front of her on the table. She broke four corn cobs into halves; she cut the carrot tops and ends, quartered the squash, snapped off the ends of the green

96

beans, and cut the cabbage into six pieces. She found the lid of a mayonnaise jar, and placed the carrot tops in it with water.

Susana was learning the rooting process in her Science class, and she was growing sweet potatoes, one avocado, pinto beans and corn in small jars in the living room. Irene added the carrot tops to the project. She glanced at the record player, its top dusty, Mariana's cleaning. Irene wiped it with her hand.

It was too hot to be cooking a *caldo;* for sure it would storm today. From her kitchen window, Irene could see the dark, black clouds, and she felt little drops of perspiration running down between her breasts and behind her neck. She prayed for rain even though she knew it would be hotter afterwards, steaming hot. She checked the meat for tenderness then added the corn. Twenty minutes later she added the carrots, fifteen minutes later, she added the green beans, squash and cabbage. Finally the *caldo* was done, and she escaped outside to sit in the breeze blowing from the Chinaberry tree.

She saw the first raindrops hit the dirt, throwing up dust. For some crazy reason she began to think of her conversation with Lorraine when she'd tried to explain her feelings with the short stories. Lightening. She remembered the class, the exam, her grade. The young girl from the left ran out to bring in her laundry before it got wet. Irene watched her move fast, her little boy running after her. The old woman from the right came out and covered some of her plants with canvas, the wind blowing her long skirt. Quickly, like when Irene had learned to connect the letters into words in the dirt, the electrical wires in her brain zapped, and she now knew what she'd been missing when she'd read the stories, what she'd tried to tell Lorraine.

She returned to the kitchen, tasted the *caldo,* then poured some soup into a small pot and went next door to the old woman's house. Irene knocked hard, insistently until the woman opened the door hesitantly, suspiciously. Irene introduced herself, gave her the soup, and stayed to talk to her. The old woman was deaf, but friendly and glad to have someone visiting her. Irene stood in front of her and spoke softly and clearly. By the time Irene left with her washed pot, Mrs. Alvarez had given her a baseball, a striped beachball and a basketball to return to Susana.

"Did you go into the witch's house?" Susana asked unbelievingly.

"She's not a witch. And the reason she never gave you back these balls is because you break her plants. She's got beautiful carnations and roses, so don't you dare throw another ball into her yard."

Irene poured soup again and took it to her other neighbor. Her name was Lillian, and she loved to go to The Loft Theatre to see foreign movies with her husband, Alfredo. By the time Irene left Lillian's house, they had arranged to babysit for each other, even though Irene wasn't too sure where she'd go.

97

And so, the following month, Irene was to report to work.

She was getting ready for her first day at work when her first visitor came. It was Mrs. Alvarez carrying a bouquet of red carnations. Irene threw out the plastic chrysanthemums and replaced them with the carnations. Mrs. Alvarez looked her over.

"You look very pretty." She touched Irene's face. "When I was young, we had curls, here, like this," she pulled the hairpins by Irene's ears, and twirled the loosened strands into curls. "Now, a flower in your hair and you will look like a flamenco dancer from Spain," she said as she cut a carnation from the bunch.

Lillian was next. She carried a Tupperware container with a slice of pecan pie for Irene's first coffee-break.

"Susana says your Mom's coming down the street," she told Irene.

Lillian, Mrs. Alvarez, and Irene walked outside. Far away they could see her mother walking slowly. When she arrived she handed Irene a red silk pouch.

"It's *la piedra imán*, a magnetic stone with ironized dirt, guaranteed to bring you luck. An amulet. Inside is a silver dime, for money; a goldpiece, for more fortune; a grain of wheat, for food; and very importantly, a *chilecote* bean, for love. Don't lose it." She turned to the other women. "I'm not superstitious, but you never know, do you?"

Irene, red flower in her hair, carrying the slice of pecan pie, and the Iman Rock in her pants' pocket, walked to the bus stop. At the corner, before she turned, she looked back and waved at the three women. They looked, Irene thought, like movie extras in a Fellini film often described by Lillian. All that was missing was a marching military band. A kettle drum, a tuba? They kept waving, and Irene went to work in the basement floor of the new City Hall, as Mail Clerk II, and with her luck, hard work and determination, Irene could, in no time at all, move up to Clerk Typist I.

Helen Marie Viramontes

The Broken Web

I.

His quick-paced footsteps sounded throughout the hollowness of
the church and grew louder as he approached the pew where she sat,
cold and chaste as the stone shapes of the holy family. Her eyes had
followed the floating silent figure of a shawlclad, shriveled woman,
performing the ritual of candlelighting, before her ears became aware of
his footsteps. The black-robed priest passed her, and soon the footsteps
dissolved into the distance. He disappeared inside the dark vacuum of
the confessional booth.

He entered the middle booth and waited for the first sign of early
morning sinners. The door to his left opened and closed. Leaning his ear
near the small black-screened window, the priest waited until he heard
the protesting creak the leather made when the heaviness of the sinner's
knee rested against it, before opening its panes.

"Bless me Father, for I have sinned. It has been four days since....."

It was always the same monotonous whisper; man and girl and boy
and woman—no real difference. They came to him seeking redemption;
they had stepped into the realm of sin; they had all slapped his walls with
hideous, ridiculously funny and often imaginary sins—and they all had
expected him to erase their sins, to ease their souls so that they could,
with the innocence of a pure heart, enter into sin once again. The
whispering tune of secrets hidden and finally banished.

"The dreams, Father, I am still having that bad dream."

"Are you dreaming unnatural acts?" He drummed his fingers on
his knees.

"I think so. At least it is to me, Father."

"Is it anything sexual?"

"No." He wasn't listening, was he? "No," she repeated. "It's like
a nightmare. I close my eyes and there is darkness. I think I'm asleep,
then....."

He heard movement.

". . . then, my eyelids become one black screen. I anticipate a movie
or something. While I am waiting, I begin to hear voices. It's my father,
talking loud, his words loud and slurred. They're arguing about something.
Something having to do with her—my mother, then . . . No. Something
having to do with my father. I still see the screen before my eyes, but I'm
so sleepy. Yreina, you knew her, Father, my younger sister, begs me to

pray to God to make the voices stop. But you see, Father, I can't because I'm asleep, and when you're asleep, you don't know what's going on. Everything is not real, and so the voices aren't real and I wanted it that way. By morning, I would open my eyes with no memory, nothing. So I wasn't supposed to know what was happening."

She stopped there, and again he heard movement.

"Go on," he heard himself say.

"I'm asleep; I see a speck on the screen. A far away speck coming closer and bigger and bigger and closer and soon the speck shapes into a statue. Our Lord with His hands outstretched. I feel comforted, even if He is only a statue in the living room. I don't hear voices. Good. I'm asleep."

Again there was silence. He hadn't had breakfast yet and his stomach gurgled in anger. She continued.

"There He stands. Solid. But what happened next I will never understand. I will never be able to forgive myself for letting it happen. I heard something, something loud. A bullet sound. It rang. The ringing visualized into a tail connected to the bullet sound. I saw it pierce the image, burst like a firecracker. Sparks. Pierce it into little pieces before my eyes, flashing light on the screen. I think I know what happened, but it's a dream. I'm asleep, you see."

He's on the couch. Please my God, he's full of blood. Wake up, Martha, quick, pleaseohmygod . . . Someone broke a statue of Jesus—the one with His hands outstretched, and now he's bleeding on the couch. I heard the crash and the bones shatter like sparks from wall to wall, but I want to be left alone. *He's bleeding all over the. . . .* I keep my eyelids cemented together and I wish I could stuff cotton balls in her volanic mouth but Yreina's an eruption. I heard the explosion, goddammit, so leave me alone. I was sinking into the mattress until I could barely see the tops of my warm sheets; then, with the burst, I was vomiting on top of them. Stay asleep. So good to sleep. I act as if Yreina is just another addition to my sleep. I feel hands, cold and tight around my neck as Yreina screams *Wakeup Martha, jesusmío, Mama shot. . . .*

II.

The saloon consisted of various kitchen tables and chairs colored from egg-yolk yellows to checkered reds and whites. Although it was the rainy mid-March season, deflated balloons and faded crepe paper remained on the ceiling as a reminder of a never-ceasing New Year celebration. Christmas lights shone against two mirrors on one wall directly behind the bar. The dance floor was a small area made up of cracked, unsettled tiles often caked with mud until Olivia cleaned them early the next morning. Olivia, the evening barmaid and morning cleaning woman of Los Amigos, mopped the floors with a thick heavy cloth connected to a mop stick. Her shoulders tired of pushpulling the mop; the ache soon dropped from her shoulders and concentrated in her legs and feet—those same dancing feet that patted the mud tighter into the cracks of the tiles.

It was the rainy season and business seemed slower than usual, for although there was still an even flow of customers, the tips dwindled to almost nothing. This time, however, Olivia didn't mind all that much; she looked forward to seeing the man that had, without knowing it, unburied her feelings of loneliness and at the same time given her anticipated pleasure by just being in the same room with her. Presently, he was the man she secretly loved.

She had not felt like this in a very long time, moonwarm and tender for another person. She loved once before, but not secretly. She lived openly with that man, bringing forth two sons. But what a scandal she, Olivia, had made. If she would have to live an outcast, she, Olivia would do so for him. He left one afternoon. The room was getting hotter.

—*Oh but could he love. Love her anywhere, anyplace.* She remembered when she thought her head had exploded and bled between her legs when he first made love to her on the roof of her house. She could remember that slow-slap, faint-slap, almost-monotonous-slap of her mother making tortillas in the kitchen right beneath them turn into an intense applause . . . and then she hated him, his two sons—thank God she gave them her name—and finally love itself. Her arms thrust the mopstick harder.

But Tomas. He was not a coward. Some day, she would have to let him know how she felt. But she couldn't—shouldn't wait too long. Already her youth was peeling off her face like the paint on the saloon walls. Olivia stopped to inspect the job. The dance floor was ready for tonight.

Olivia thought of her two sons as she locked the front doors of the saloon, proud of herself for being the only other person to hold the key to the establishment, and she smiled that smile when she remembered the roof incident. The key: just her and the old man. The old, tight, stinky sonofabitch, she thought. It was noon and the streets of Tijuana were flooded with puddles of muddy water. Two kids bathed near the street corner and the Saturday tourists waved like national flags along the sidewalks. The air was unusually fresh and she looked up at the sky. It will be a good night tonight she thought as she hurried home.

Tomas' wife was a statue-tall woman with floods of thick black hair that reached to the folds of her buttocks. She watched her reflection in the mirror; brushing her hair with slow-moving strokes, she enjoyed the luxury of time and the full view of herself. It was like a vacation long

101

deserved to stay at a place where she didn't have to make beds, or endlessly fight the dirt-attracting floor, or worry about feeding the family. Although he did not bring her on his trips across the border to Tijuana (using the excuse that it would be dangerous for her since she would probably be jailed along with him if he were ever caught passing Mexicanos without proper papers), he asked her to come as far as Chula Vista. Perhaps he thought she needed the rest from her duties as wife and mother, and only in complete solitude did she feel like a woman. Too soon would the grape harvest return; the Fresno sun was almost mockingly waiting to bleed the sweat from all five of them. All five. *Mis niños*. Next time she would bring Martha, and Miguelito. She braided her hair. He had gone attending business in Tijuana and would not be back for two hours. He would pick her up later and they would go to the saloon tonight. Tomas' wife wondered if that old barmaid (what-was-her-name-now?) still worked there and she wondered if Tomas left her would she become like her? Weary of travel, she rested her body on the fresh-sheeted soft bed.

Olivia had always avoided looking at herself completely in the mirror; her eyes focused only on the part she attended to. She knew age was nesting. The short skirt revealed her skinny legs that knotted at the knees, and her small but protruding belly surpassed her breasts. Yet she tried making the best of it; with a low-cut blouse and wearing her hair down, she would not be called a vieja so often. Like an artist, she began creating her illusionary eyes with the colors of a forest.

Tomas' wife dreamt of houses. Big ones that would belong to all five of them. A color T.V. and an island. She dreamt of her mother; dozens of diapers blazing, and an invisible bird with huge wings.

Two large false lashes were glued expertly on her natural ones. The eyes were traced with liner and the eyelids finely painted with eye shadows. Done. She lit a cigarette and sat in front of the mirror, re-evaluating the masterpiece. Now, not even the make-up covered her deeper wrinkles. She put her cigarette down, wet her fingers with her tongue, and rubbed away the chappedness of her arms.

Tomas' wife stretched out slowly, awakening like a cat. It was later than she had anticipated; she hurried to unbraid her hair and continued brushing it as he entered the room, carrying a bag of sweet bread, two bright pink and green ponchos wrapped in transparent paper, and a toy rifle, resembling his own, for Miguelito.

For the niños. Tomorrow we have to leave early. Next week, I must return. Only then will the gente be ready and waiting at Los Amigos. To Tomas' wife this meant that he would not take her across the border and into Tijuana. She understood him well, although he said nothing; her vacation was cut short. He laid the purchases on the bed and went into the bathroom. There was the flush sound of the toilet, then the rush of water of the shower. She put her hair up in a bun, disrobed, and entered the shower with him discreetly.

The perfume was the final touch. Olivia left some tacos and three dollars on the kitchen table. She never knew exactly when her sons came home nor when she herself would, so she left food and money always. It was a silent contract that they had with one another; she never played mother and they, in turn, never asked her to. Olivia blessed herself, sighed, and hurried to the saloon anticipating Tomas' laugh.

III.

The promise of night disappeared. He would probably awaken disoriented and bewildered at the unfamiliar room, she thought. But she would assure him that nothing happened because nothing did happen. Tomas had sunk onto the cracked dance floor tile after that last shot of Jose Cuervo, drunk, and she had asked his companions to take him to her place. Tomorrow he was leaving to Fresno, to his wife, and who knew when she would see him again. Tomas—buried beneath the blankness that liquor caused—slept soundly, unyielding to the fingers that petted and comforted him.

Olivia undressed and lay close to him, defeated but warm. The heaviness of his slow breathing and his oppressive presence held blocks against her sleep. She rested her hand against the firm folds of his breasts crushing his unraveled curls; her hand caught the rhythm of his breath. She heard the Sunday morning church bells summon the mourning sleepless women with dust on their hair, and she would have to wake him before the dawn revealed her secret. Today he was returning to Fresno.

"Tomas." She hoped to awaken him but all he did was grunt and jerk away from her. The bells of the church rang heavy in the air. Olivia touched his shoulder.

"Tomas." The bells faded. "Sometimes in my sleep," she whispered to him as if speaking to a child not yet born of its senses, ". . . I can see the inside of me. Mesh. It looks like mesh. Pieces of bones rattling like ice in an empty glass. Those are times I wish I was an artist so I could paint a picture of myself . . ." Olivia closed her eyes. ". . . lime-light green, dull yellow, mixed together like vomit." She turned away from him, facing the window. The cool awakening gray-glow dawn illuminated slowly.

"It's true, Tomas. It's true," she whispered to the window. "Sometimes in your sleep you can see the inside of you." His snoring was like the soft hum of a bee next to her ears. She became still, almost tranquil as that morning, and her eyes bled tears, first quiet flowing tears, then hot, salty stab tears uncontrolled, while his snoring was like the soft hum of a bee next to her ears.

IV.

"Rave, rave, you woman—you guiltless one? You, the very counterfeiter, you whorish bitch. Stay, sit, before I strike you again. And again, but you will not cry in front of me, will you? You will not please me by unveiling your pain, will you? Let them hear, they're probably not mine anyway.

"The marijuana opiates, the liquor seduces. That is why nothing can hurt me, not even you. I work to live, and I hate it. I live for you, and I hate it. I have another shot of tequila—tequila is a good mistress—and two more before I ask myself, why live?

"I loved you too much that now I have no pride, no respect for myself. I await the breeze that will lift and carry me away from you.

"Ha. Ha. That I, you say, am unfaithful to you? In Tijuana, last week? Even you, like the devil, disguise yourself as a gnat to spy on me? I should have spied on you that night you let him rip the virginity out of you, the blood and slime of your innocence trailing down the sides of his mouth. You tramp. You righteous cruel, cruelest bitch. Have I no right to be unfaithful? Weren't you? Vete mucho a chingar a tu madre, más cabrona que la chingada . . ."

Martha, please pray to God to make them stop. God doesn't listen to me.

. . . Perra, don't rage to me about that barmaid! Answer me, vieja cabrona, ans—Like a drowning, hissing fire, his ghost smoldered while he lay there. Tomas' wife thought of towers crumbling and then of his intoxicants that unleash and loosen those hidden passions that burn through the soul and float up into a belch of clouds, smothering and causing them to rage, that pure rage that no one really knew of. Tomas was now an invincible cloud of past, she thought. A coiled smoking ghost. She kneeled beside him, laying her puzzle-piece heart against his unliving one. Unliving because she had pressured the trigger tight, then tightfingered it until his chest blew up, spilling the oozing blood that stained all tomorrows. And yet he seemed more alive. No. More real than anything, anyone around her. She spoke to him with the voice of prayer, "And you? The choice was yours, Tomas. As for me, I had no choice. I had given up being a woman for you, just like you gave up your own respect and dignity when you married me. Surely now, at this moment, I feel so close to you, equally dead, but equally real." How could she explain to him that she was so tired and wrinkled and torn by him, his God, and his word? She had tried to defy the rules by sleeping with another man, but that only left her worse off. And she could not leave him because she no longer owned herself. He owned her, her children owned her, and she needed them all to live. And she was tired of needing.

What to tell the police, what to say? Tomas' unfaithfulness. That was as real as his body on the couch. "Tomas was a trustful man, but flesh is flesh, men are men . . ."

The acid fumes that fiercely clawed her insides crept timidly away from her and mingled with the roaming urinal scent of the jail cell. Her children in time would forgive her. But God? He would never understand. He was a man, too. No. She would become a cricket wailing nightly for redemption. That suited her, she would be wailing for redemption. With the strength of defiant resignation, she stared, wide-eyed and zombie-like at the name printed on the wristband.

V.

"She moaned a lot in her sleep and sometimes she'd say things out loud that she'd never say awake. Since we slept on the same bed, she would sometimes hang onto me and call me by his name. It wasn't your father's name though; it wasn't Tomas.

"Under other circumstances, if you had asked me these questions I would have belted you hard, as I often did to curious children who peeked through my window. I am old now, old and with the same name and I tell you these things because soon you will be ready for marriage and the worms will cover me completely and it'll be too late to tell you anything. How uncomfortable, these worms; today I found two of them squirming around my toes. Yesterday I found one burrowing into my thigh. I kill them, but I am losing my strength.

"I am not an evil woman, Martha, but my body has suffered much. Look at his body—twisted like tangled tree roots. Hand me that glass of water, Martita, I am dry. A little warm, but good. So you want to know about your parents? Damn fly. Flies drop dead all around this house. Just the other day, one fell into my teeth glass. For God's life, I couldn't bring myself to put on my teeth. Wretched things, these teeth.

"As you know, I am your oldest aunt. Because I was the first, our mother—not knowing how many daughters she would have—saved the beauty that was supposed to be shared among us. Since I was the first-born daughter, she gave me good teeth, and since your mother was the last, she gave her all the beauty she denied her other daughters including me, but at least I had good teeth. I remember an old boyfriend of mine. Alejandro? No Alfredo. Alfredo was his name. He used to tell me 'Smile, Chica—smile, so I can see my reflection. He was a good man, that Alfredo. You know, Martha, Alfredo and I were going to get married once. I knew him for years and years and he always called me Little Rabbit because of my teeth. But once he began to notice your mother's developing breasts, and that look I often caught her giving him, I told him to go far away. He was a good man, that Alfredo.

"It is already getting dark. Please light Jesucristo's candle for me. The days seem so short now. You will say a rosary with me before you go to sleep, won't you? What did you say? What was your father doing all this time? Tempting the dreams of older women, that Tomas. I had my eye out for him long before his voice even changed. But your mother gave him the look, and I had no right to tell him to go away. From the very beginning, he gave himself completely to her. And that was a mistake. Because her heart was just a seed then, she could not give him something she had not yet created. This drove Tomas crazy and I would tell her, tell her 'it is evil to make him suffer,' and your mother would say, 'I can't help it if he loves me.' He asked me to watch over your mother, that Tomas.

"Jesúsmío but it gets cold in here. My body begins to freeze at the feet and by morning I am a snow cone. Thank you for the blanket, Martita. Now where was . . . oh. Many weeks pass. One late night—did I tell you that we shared a bed, your mother and I? Well, one late night I hear tapping on the window. I think it's Tomas coming to get her and I act as if nothing awakes me. Your mother slips out from between the sheets like a snake shedding its skin. She opens the window and they exchange whispers. It is a man all right, but not Tomas.

"God have mercy on my soul, child, but you are a good Martita who must know the truth or else you'll never be at peace and this is why I hope I am not wrong in telling you.

"The man apparently waited outside while your mother felt around the dark room for her robe. I burst out in loud whispers asking her where she is going and who is that man. 'I'll return,' is what she answers. After a long while I am awakened by a cold weight smelling of soft dirt and grass. It was her, breathing as if she had run for miles. Tomas returned about three months after and I, though years paint coats of vagueness on memories, will never forget the look on Tomas' face when your mother greeted him on the porch with a small belly. They got married a few days later.

"Do you hear the crickets? Our mother warned us against killing crickets because they are the souls of condemned people. Do you hear their wailing, Martita? They conduct the mass of dead only at night. You will say a rosary with me tonight, won't you?"

Nicholasa Mohr

An Awakening . . . Summer 1956

for Hilda Hidalgo

The young woman looked out of the window as the greyhound bus sped by the barren, hot, dry Texas landscape. She squinted, clearing her vision against the blazing white sunlight. Occasionally, she could discern small adobe houses clumped together like mushrooms, or a gas station and diner standing alone and remote in the flat terrain. People were not visible. They were hiding, she reasoned, seeking relief indoors in the shade. How different from her native Puerto Rico, where luscious plants, trees and flowers were abundant. Green was the color of that Island, soothing, cool, inviting. And people were seen everywhere, living, working, enjoying the outdoors. All of her life had been spent on her beloved land. For more than a decade she had been in service of the church. Now, this was a new beginning. After all, it had been her choice, her sole decision to leave. At the convent school where she had been safe and loved, they had reluctantly bid her farewell with an open invitation to return. Leaving there had been an essential part of working it all out, she thought, one had to start somewhere. Still, as she now looked out at all the barrenness before her, she felt a stranger in a foreign land and completely alone.

She was on her way to spend the summer with her good friend Ann. They were going to discuss the several directions in which she might continue to work. After all, she had skills; her degrees in elementary education and a master's in counseling. There was also the opportunity offered her of that scholarship toward a doctorate in Ohio. The need to experience the world independently, without the protection of the church, was far more compelling than her new apprehension of the "unknown."

The young woman checked her wristwatch.

"On time . . ." she whispered, and settled back in her seat.

Her friend Ann was now a social worker with the working poor and the Mexican American community in a small town in rural Texas. The invitation to spend most of this summer with Ann and her family had appealed to the young woman, and she had accepted with gratitude.

"You know you are welcome to stay with us for just as long as you want," Ann had written. "You will be like another member of the family."

The knowledge that she would once more be with her good friend, discussing ideas and planning for the future, just as they had done as co-workers back home, delighted and excited her.

"Clines-Corners . . ." the bus driver announced. The next stop would be hers.

"Now, please wait at the bus depot, don't wander off. Promise to stay put, in case of a change in schedule, and we will pick you up," Ann had cautioned in her last letter.

"Sentry!" the bus driver shouted as the bus came to a sudden halt. She jumped down and the bus sped off barely missing a sleeping dog that had placed itself comfortably under the shade of a large roadside billboard. The billboard picture promised a cool lakeside ride on a motorboat, if one smoked mentholated cigarettes.

She found herself alone and watched a cloud of dust settle into the landscape as the bus disappeared into the horizon. She approached the depot building where two older Mexican men and a young black man, laborers, sat shaded on a wooden porch, eating lunch. She smiled and waved as she passed them. They nodded in response.

Inside at the ticket booth, a tall man with very pink skin peered out at her from under a dark green sun visor.

"Good day," she cleared her throat. The man nodded and waited. "I was wondering . . . eh, if there was some message for me?"

"What?" he asked.

Feeling self conscious and embarrassed, she repeated her question, adding. "I'm sorry, but it is that my English is not too perfect. I am not used to speaking English very often."

"What's you name? I can't know if there's a message for you if I don't know your name." She told him, speaking clearly and spelling each letter with care.

"Nope," he shook his head, "ain't nothing here for nobody by that name." The man turned away and continued his work.

The young woman stood for a moment wondering if her friends had received her wire stating she would arrive several hours earlier than expected. Checking the time she realized it was only twelve thirty. They were not expecting her until five in the late afternoon. She walked to the pay phone and dialed Ann's number. She waited as it rang for almost two full minutes before she replaced the receiver. Disappointed, she approached the clerk again.

"Excuse me, sir . . . can I please leave my luggage for a while? There is not an answer where my friends are living."

The man motioned her to a section of luggage racks.

"Cost you fifty cents for the first three hours, and fifteen cents for each hour after that. Pay when you come back." He handed her a soiled blue ticket.

108

"Thank you very much. Is there a place for me to get a cold drink? It is very hot . . . and I was riding on the bus for a long time."

"There's a Coke machine by the garage, right up the street. Can't miss it."

"Well, I would like a place to sit down. I think I saw a small restaurant up on the main street when I got off the bus."

"Miss, you'd be better off at the Coke machine. Soda's nice and cold. You can come back and drink it in here if you like." He looked at the young woman for a moment, nodded, and returned once more to his work.

She watched him somewhat confused and shrugged, then walked out into the hot empty street. Two mangy, flea-bitten mutts streaked with oil spots walked up to her wagging their tails.

"Bueno . . ." she smiled, "you must be my welcoming committee." They followed her as she continued up the main street. The barber shop and the hardware store were both closed. Out to lunch, she said to herself, and a nice siesta . . . now that's sensible.

Playful shouts and shrieking laughter emanated from a group of Mexican children. They ran jumping and pushing a large metal hoop. She waved at them. Abruptly, they stopped, looking with curiosity and mild interest at this stranger. They glanced at each other and, giggling, quickly began once more to run and play their game. In a moment they were gone, heading into a shaded side street.

The red and white sign above the small store displayed in bold printed letters: NATHANS FOOD AND GROCERIES—EAT IN OR TAKE OUT. On the door a smaller sign read, OPEN. Thankful, she found herself inside, enjoying the coolness and serenity of the small cafe. Two tables set against the wall were empty and except for a man seated at the counter, all the stools were unoccupied. No one else was in sight. She took a counter seat a few stools away from the man. After a minute or two, when no one appeared, the young woman cleared her throat and spoke.

"Pardon me . . . somebody. Please, is somebody here?" She waited and before she could speak again, she heard the man seated at the counter shout:

"ED! Hey Ed, somebody's out here. You got a customer!"

A middle-aged portly man appeared from the back. When he saw the young woman, he stopped short, hesitating. Slowly he walked up to her and silently stared.

"Good day," she said. "How are you?" The man now stood with his arms folded quite still without replying. "Can I please have a Pepsi-Cola." Managing a smile, she continued, "It is very hot outside, but I am sure you know that . . ."

He remained still, keeping his eyes on hers. The young woman glanced around her not quite sure what to do next. Then, she cleared her throat and tried again.

"A Pepsi-Cola, cold if you please . . ."

"Don't have no Pepsi-Colas," he responded loudly.

She looked around and saw a full fountain service, and against the rear wall, boxes filled with Pepsi-Colas.

"What's that?" she asked, confused.

The man gestured at the wall directly behind her. "Can't you read English."

Turning, she saw the sign he had directed her to. In large black letters and posted right next to the door she read:

NO COLOREDS

NO MEXICANS

NO DOGS

WILL BE SERVED ON THESE

PREMISES

All the blood in her body seemed to rush to her head. She felt her tongue thicken and her fingers turn as cold as ice cubes. Another white man's face appeared from the kitchen entrance and behind him stood a very black woman peering nervously over his shoulder.

The silence surrounding her stunned her as she realized at the moment all she was—a woman of dark olive complexion, with jet black hair; she spoke differently from these people. Therefore, she was all those things on that sign. She was also a woman alone before these white men. Jesus and the Virgin Mary . . . what was she supposed to do? Colors flashed and danced before her embracing the angry faces and cold hateful eyes that stared at her daring her to say another word. Anger and fear welled up inside her, and she felt threatened even by the shadows set against the bright sun; they seemed like daggers menacing her very existence. She was going to fight, she was not going to let them cast her aside like an animal. Deeply she inhaled searching for her voice, for her composure, and without warning, she heard herself shouting.

"I WOULD LIKE A PEPSI-COLA, I SAID! AND, I WANT IT NOW . . . RIGHT NOW!!" The words spilled out in loud rasps. She felt her heart lodged in her throat, and swallowed trying to push it back down so that she could breathe once more.

"Can't you read . . . girl?" the man demanded.

"I WANT A PEPSI. DAMN IT . . . NOW!" With more boldness, this time her voice resounded, striking the silence with an explosion. Taking out her change purse she slammed several coins on the counter. "NOW!" she demanded staring at the man. "I'm not leaving until I get my drink."

As the young woman and the middle-aged portly man stared, searching each others' eyes, that moment seemed an eternity to her. All she was, all she would ever be, was here right now at this point in time. And so she stood very still, barely blinking and concentrated, so that not

110

one muscle in her body moved.

He was the first to move. Shaking his head, he smiled and with slow deliberate steps walked over to the cases by the wall and brought back a bottle of Pepsi-Cola, placing it before her. As she picked up the bottle, she felt the heat of the liquid; it was almost too hot to hold.

"Very well," she said, surprised at the calmness in her voice. "May I please have an opener?"

"Girl . . . we ain't got no openers here. Now you got your damned drink . . . that's it. Get the hell out of here!" He turned, ignoring her, and began to work arranging cups behind the counter.

Her eyes watched him and just for an instant the young woman hesitated before she stood, grabbed the bottle and lifted it high above her bringing it down with tremendous force and smashing it against the counter edge. Like hailstones in a storm, pieces of glass flew in every direction, covering the counter and the space around her. The warm bubbling liquid drenched her. Her heavy breathing sucked in the sweetness of the cola.

"KEEP THE CHANGE!" she shouted. Quickly she slammed the door behind her and once again faced the heat and the empty street.

She walked with her back straight and her head held high.

"BITCH!" she could hear his voice. "YOU DAMNED MEXICAN COLORED BITCH! CAN'T TREAT YOU PEOPLE LIKE HUMAN BEINGS . . . you no good . . ."

His voice faded as she walked past the main street, the bus depot and the small houses of the town. After what seemed a long enough time, she stopped, quite satisfied she was no longer in that town near that awful hateful man. The highway offered no real shade, and so she turned down a side road. There the countryside seemed gentler, a few trees and bushes offered some relief. A clump of bushes up on a mound of earth surrounded a maple tree that yielded an oasis of cool shade. She climbed up the mound and sat looking about her. She enjoyed the light breeze and the flight of large crows that dotted the sky in the distance. The image of the man and what had happened stirred in her a sense of humiliation and hurt. Tears clouded her view and she began to cry quietly at first, and then her sobs got louder. Intense rage overtook her and her sobbing became screams that pierced the quiet countryside. After a while, her crying subsided and she felt a sharp pain in her hand. She looked down and realized she still clenched tightly the neck of the broken Pepsi-Cola bottle. The jagged edges of glass had penetrated in between her thumb and forefinger; she was still bleeding. Releasing her grip, the young woman found a handkerchief in her pocket. Carefully she pressed it to the wound and in moments the bleeding stopped. Exhausted, she closed her eyes, leaned against the tree, and fell asleep.

She dreamt of that cool lakeside and the motorboat on the billboard, that might take her back home to safety and comfort. Friends would be there, waiting, protection hers just for the asking.

"Wake up . . . it's all right. It's me, Ann." She felt a hand on her shoulder and opened her eyes. Ann was there, her eyes filled with kindness and concern. Again, the young woman cried, openly and without shame, as she embraced her friend.

"I know, we got your wire, but only after we got home. By then it was late, around three o'clock, and we went looking for you right away. This a very small town. You caused quite a stir. I should have warned you about things out here. But, I thought it would be best to tell you when we were together. I'm so sorry . . . but don't worry . . . you are safe and with us. We are proud of you . . . the way you stood up . . . but, never mind that now. Let's get you home where you can rest. But, you were wonderful. . . ."

In the weeks that followed, the young woman worked with Ann. She made lifetime friends in the small Texas community. There were others like her and like Ann, who would fight against those signs. Civil rights had to be won and the battles still had to be fought. She understood quite clearly in that summer of 1956, that no matter where she might settle, or in which direction life would take her, the work she would commit herself to, and indeed her existence itself, would be dedicated to the struggle and the fight against oppression. Consciously for the very first time in her life, the young woman was proud of all she was, her skin, her hair and the fact that she was a woman.

Riding back East on the bus, she looked at her hand and realized the wound she had suffered had healed. However, two tiny scars remained, quite visible.

"A reminder . . . should I ever forget," she whispered softly.

Settling back, she let the rhythmic motion of the large bus lull her into a sweet sleep. The future with all its uncertainties was before her; now she was more than ready for this challenge.

La Doctora Barr

My earliest memory is of when I was about three, when my brother Joey was born. Joey was delivered at home by 'la Doctora Barr' who had also delivered me. She practiced medicine in the nearby city of *Burbanke*, as we called Burbank, and also came to the homes of *la gente mexicana* of Pacoima to dispense medicine and deliver babies.

She was of medium height, a bit plump, with soft brown hair worn in a bun from which wispy tendrils escaped to form a halo around her cheerful face. She wore little makeup; she needed none for her ruddy, healthy cheeks were a bright red so that when she smiled it appeared she had two apples for cheeks. She wore glasses with wire frames which often slipped to her nose so that she appeared to peer at us in a friendly way.

"Well, playing ball again I see."

"Sí Señora Barr." "Yes Mrs. Doctor." "Oh yes ma'am."

"And are you helping your mother at home?"

"Yes ma'am, I wash dishes, sweep the kitchen and make the beds."

"Liar, I make the beds."

"No she doesn't, I do. She makes them too messy—I have to make them over," I would protest to *la doctora* as she disappeared into the doorway of a nearby house.

Most of the time Dr. Barr would not be consulted by the expectant mother until the pregnancy was well into its final month. Most of the women had an idea of what to do during *un embarazo*. The women continued with their work, caring for home and children until the first labor pains would signal an imminent birth. A neighbor was first alerted, she in turn would notify *un señor* who would rush off to the one public phone booth located on Van Nuys Boulevard to call the doctor. In the meantime the neighbor women would bring out *sábanas limpias*, put water to boil and farm the kids out to neighbors or relatives so as to spare them the confusion that accompanied *un parto*, as at times the younger children slept in the same room as the parents, even shared the same bed; thus it was neither advisable nor practical to have them around.

When Dr. Barr arrived all was in readiness; the expectant mother lay on clean, white sheets, her face washed, hair combed back in a *chongo* or *una trenza,* in her hand, a clean rag to bite on when the pain became unbearable as it was thought to be *muy ranchera* to scream out. The *señoras* made sure *una botella de alcohol, toallas limpias* and a pan for the afterbirth were nearby along with a supply of clean white rags to be used as sanitary napkins as few women of the *barrio* could afford to buy this item at *la Tienda Blanca*, an item not to be found *en la tienda de Don Jesús*.

Not all of the women believed in a scientific approach to childbirth; among these was a neighbor *la Juana*, said to be *una india* because of her dark skin, high cheekbones, black slanted eyes, and the facility for delivering babies every nine months without a fuss. *La Juana* never 'showed' until she was in her eighth month; somehow she carried her babies in such a manner that her stomach did not protrude.

One time I was playing ball with my best friend Chelo, when her mother was summoned to help *la Juana* who was about to give birth.

"Doña Placencia, Doña Placencia, dice la Juana que ya es tiempo."

"Avísale que ya voy."

Upon hearing this exchange Chelo and I quickly volunteered to help carry the towels and alcohol as we were curious to be around someone who was about the give birth, a subject that was discussed by our mothers with sighs of *Jesús, María y José*—and ended abruptly when we were within earshot. Once at the house we were not allowed inside but chose to remain outside in hopes of being asked inside or to run *un mandado*. Chelo and I soon got bored waiting for something to happen. We left but later returned on the pretext of wanting permission to go to *la Tienda de Don Jesús*. Chelo's mother pretended to be pleased at our request since we never asked but *told* her where we were going, only her smiling eyes gave her away. She quickly let us in—as she went to find the handkerchief where she kept her money rolled in a tight knot. While Chelo stood and waited for her mother to return *con un cinco*, I tiptoed into the next room and peeked inside the bedroom. The room was dark; I could barely make out the figures of two women, *la Juana*, bent over, a woman standing immediately behind her, towels at her feet, hands outstretched.

"Puje, puje, un poquito más."

"Ay, cómo duele."

"Pues eso ya sabía—si no es el primero."

"Ya sé . . . ojalá sea el último."

"Sí, pero primero pújele."

I stood mesmerized, staring into the room, trying to see more but was forced to move quickly into the next room when I heard Chelo's mother approaching from another direction. She gave me a look that spoke volumes; I believe she saw me coming out of the room. However she said nothing, handed Chelo two dimes, then quickly shooed us out the door. Later that evening we heard that a son had been born to Juana. Early the next day she was seen outside, new baby strapped to her back, hanging clothes on the line, looking not as if she had just given birth. The *señoras* of the neighborhood shook their heads in wonder (and disgust) at *los modos rancheros de la Juana* who neither asked for *la doctora* nor

114

followed *la dieta* afterwards.

One of the areas of conflict experienced by Dr. Barr and the women of our barrio dealt with the special diet that new mothers were supposed to follow. *La Dieta* pertained not only to diet but to after-care following a birth. For all her goodness, Dr. Barr would become exasperated when her patients insisted on following the traditions and customs inherent in Mexican culture rather than her own instructions, which she felt were more scientific and "wholesome." Dr. Barr encouraged *las señoras* to bathe and wash their hair soon after *un parto;* however Mexican custom dictated otherwise. In order not to catch *frío,* a woman was supposed to refrain from bathing for at least six weeks. Along with this, the new mother should avoid eating certain foods such as *limones,* avocados y *carne de puerco;* foods that would sour her milk. In addition the new mother was made to wear a heavy *banda* around her stomach, a band made of old sheets cut into strips which was wound around her stomach immediately after she had expelled the afterbirth and which was expected to remain for the same six weeks to ensure that *la matriz* would quickly contract and return to its normal size. Heavy lifting was prohibited as was heavy housework such as the washing of clothes *en el lavadero,* the mopping of floors and hanging washclothes on the line. This then was a time when a woman like my mother who worked hard most of her life was allowed to rest and be waited on by family and neighbors. However in time the custom of *la dieta* was either modified or abolished as not everyone could afford the luxury of lying in bed for six weeks. In time the younger women wanted to be *como las americanas* and soon did as *la doctora* suggested: got up on the third day, took a bath and continued with their daily chores. It seems that *la Juana,* an illiterate woman, knew what she was doing all along.

Mary Helen Ponce

Recuerdo: How I changed the war and won the game.

During World War II I used to translate the English newspaper's war news for our adopted grandmother Doña Luisa and her friends. All of them were *señoras de edad,* elderly ladies who could not read English, only their native Spanish.

Every afternoon they would gather on Doña Luisa's front porch to await Doña Trinidad's son who delivered the paper to her promptly at 5 p.m. There, among the *geranios* and pots of *yerba buena* I would bring them the news of the war.

At first I enjoyed doing this, for the *señoras* would welcome me as a grown-up. They would push their chairs around in a semicircle, the better to hear me. I would sit in the middle, on a *banquito* that was a milk crate. I don't remember how I began to be their translator but because I was an obedient child and at eight a good reader, I was somehow coerced or selected.

I would sit down, adjust my dress, then slowly unwrap the paper, reading the headlines to myself in English, trying to decide which news items were the most important, which to tell first. Once I had decided, I would translate them into my best Spanish for Doña Luisa and her friends.

The news of a battle would bring sighs of *Jesús, María y José, Ay Díos Mío,* from the ladies. They would roll their eyes toward heaven, imploring our Lord to protect their loved ones from danger. In return they vowed to light candles or to make a *manda,* a pilgrimage to *la Virgen de San Juan* in the nearby town of Sunland. Once I had read them the highlights of the war I was allowed to play ball with my friends.

One day we had an important ball game going, our team was losing, and it was my turn at bat. Just then Doña Luisa called me. It was time for *las noticias.* Furious at this interruption yet not daring to disobey, I dropped the bat, ran to the porch, ripped open the paper, pointed to the headlines and in a loud voice proclaimed: "Ya están los japoneses en San Francisco . . . los esperan en Los Angeles muy pronto," or "The Japanese have landed in San Francisco; they should be in Los Angeles soon."

"*Jesús, María y José, Sangre de Cristo, Ave María Purísima*" chanted las señoras as I dashed off to resume my game. "*Díos mío ya vámonos, ya vámonos*" they said as chairs were pushed aside, "*vamos a la Iglesia . . . a rezarle al Señor.*"

After that I was able to translate according to whim—and depending on whether or not I was up to bat when the paper arrived.

Mary Helen Ponce

Recuerdo: Los piojos

As a child in the barrio of Pacoima, my best friends were *la Nancy* who had changed her name from Natcha and thought she was "so big," *la Virgie* who had got into a fight with Meño M. and had lost, only to be spanked *con el cinto* by her father for fighting and *por andar en la calle jugando con muchachos*, and *la Chelo* who lived across the street from me.

Chelo was considered timid by almost everyone in the neighborhood, especially the adults, for she never talked back to anyone. She, like the rest of our generation of Mexican-Americans, was intimidated by the Anglo world, especially at school where at times we felt like second-class citizens with our funny customs, hard-to-pronounce names and our bad English and where we were constantly told, "Speak English, English only, we're not in Mexico now." While some of the braver students such as *la Nancy* would give a smart retort, Chelo would just hang her head and say nothing.

It seems we lived in two worlds, the secure *barrio* that comforted and accepted us and the "Other," the institutions such as school that were out to acculturate us, sanitize, Americanize and de-lice us at least once a year, usually in spring when everything hatched, including lice.

During the spring months just after the new semester started in early February, we were checked for immunizations, tonsillitis and for symptoms of whatever disease was prevalent such as *el sarampión o la tos ferina*. At times we thought that the blessing of the throats that occurred in February was not a coincidence, that perhaps God was aware that we needed special protection from the school nurse.

We cringed when we were called to the nurse's office for she was forever inspecting our ears, mouth and hair. She would dab smelly purple stuff on any area that looked infected. We hated the smell of iodine, of the medicine that refused to wash off and which we felt marked us as "diseased," for we had often overheard the teachers discuss us, our sicknesses and funny customs:

"My stars! Did you say your girls were scratching their hair?"

"Dear me yes, it's that time of year you know, what else do you expect, them living like they do, sleeping in one bed—nits do jump you know."

"My stars! You'd think they would keep their hair short, make it easier to get rid of them."

"You know how they are, just crazy about long hair. Must be the culture—just like bad teeth and that t.b."

"My land, I swear I just disinfect myself ever so carefully."

117

It seemed that lice were part of our culture, along with poverty, shabby homes, low-paying jobs and "too, too many children." It seemed that we Mexican-Americans, as we were then called, had so many things wrong with us we wondered why it was that we were remotely happy. We lived in a loving home, attended school, played *a las escondidas*, enjoyed the *jamaicas*, attended catechism—lived what we thought was a good life. We felt content at home and could not understand why we had to be singled out as a group when it was suspected that one of us had lice.

One time when I was in third grade at Pacoima Elementary several girls thought to have nits had been rounded up and marched to the school nurse. When word got around that *nits* had been found on several girls, many of us cringed for we knew that we would all be suspect and forced to be inspected whether we liked it or not. Just to be suspected of having *piojos* was in itself a disgrace. On this day the third graders were inspected room by room. The nurse would carefully part our hair then peer into the strands of hair, check the back of our heads, then give us a shove towards the teacher who would smile and at times hand us that tattle-tale yellow paper which we would pin onto our dress—a note that our Spanish-speaking parents could not read but which they knew meant they would have to take steps to de-lice their child. We dreaded having even a speck of dirt or dandruff, for to the eagle-eyed nurse everything that was visible on our dark hair was suspect.

On this day when it was our room's turn, we all marched off to the nurse. Chelo's room was ahead of us and so we began to talk as we waited.

"I hate it."

"Me too."

"*Qué vergüenza*."

"Simona vieja panzona."

"Shut up."

"You shut up *mocosa*."

"Babosa."

"Piojenta."

"Tú."

"Tú."

When it was Chelo's turn she began to sniffle, for more than once she had been found to have nits. She hesitated, looked around for an ally; finding none she reluctantly stepped forward as the nurse called out "Consuelo Lopez." Because the nurse and teacher were whispering to each other, Chelo stood and waited, then the nurse turned to her and very carefully picked up a *trenza* with the tip of her fingers and began to peer into it. Unfortunately for Chelo the nurse spotted something white for she quickly pushed her away toward "la Mrs. Eddington" who gave her the yellow slip as though offering a reward for having suffered through this ordeal. Chelo was dismissed and sent to her room along

118

with other girls who also were sniffling. When it was my turn I stepped forward like a defiant lamb not quite ready for the sacrifice.

"Mary Helen Ponce."

"Here."

"Hummm, are you Josephine's sister?"

"Yes ma'am."

"And Connie's?"

"Yes ma'am, and Isabelle's and Cora's too. They're all my sisters," I answered.

"Well, I doubt very much if you have lice, so far we haven't found any on your sisters—you may be excused." "Next."

"But I want to be inspected."

"Nonsense child, there's no need, you look clean enough," intoned the nurse as she gave me a shove towards the line.

"But I itch."

"What? Itch where, just what do you mean?"

"Here in my head," I answered, then proceeded to scratch my Shirley Temple curls, "right here."

"Tell me, do you play with anyone with lice?"

"Yes ma'am," I answered proudly, "Consuelo Lopez is my best friend."

"Well, fancy that, now I suppose you got them from her."

"Yes, I mean no ma'am, I just itch," was my lame reply as I waited to be handed a yellow slip. Mrs. Eddington was trying not to laugh as she told me to go to the room. The nurse just snorted and said "Next." "Could I have one of those?" I said. "Next," said she.

In the hallway I encountered my classmates, Chelo among them, all smiling for we were once again together and found consolation among ourselves. We smiled as we walked to the room, for the *vergüenza* was over, we had survived another inspection which we would later talk about as "an event." It was time to return to our schoolwork, to try to pretend we were like the children in the books who played with "Spot" and had never heard of lice. We knew that this experience was part of our culture, part of being a Mexican-American, sort of like having black hair and brown eyes. The inspection went with our identity as did the yellow slips we wore home as a badge of honor.

Later, when Chelo and I walked home she refused to play the pushing game we usually played on the way home. I put my arm around her, like best friends and tried to make her smile but she was not in a mood for fun. Chelo knew she would have to endure the smelly *petrolio* that was the only remedy to kill lice, a smell that lingered and made her dizzy.

Later, when she had been de-liced and shampooed with the Packers Pine Tar Soap we all used, she and I once again played together, both at school and at home, black heads pressed together, sharing secrets, sharing life.

119

Las Mujeres de los Revolucionarios   *Santa Barraza*

120

Yo Como Canuta　　　　　　　　　　　*Santa Barraza*

Alma-En-Pena

Tus ojos verán cosas extrañas y
hablarás sin concierto.
Proverbios, 23, 33.

Cuando me lo contó, la miré sorprendido, más bien asustado,
¡carajo!, no fuera que estuiera volviéndose loca como sus dos tías, la
prima Elena y su propia madre. Desde ese día vivo observándola, por
supuesto, sin que ella se dé cuenta. Sospecha algo, porque a menudo se
vuelve a mí repentina y sorpresivamente para atraparme en el acto de
espiarla. Pero como siempre, me encuentra hundido en el periódico,
lejos, en España, envuelto en las protestas estudiantiles contra la policía
armada que invade las aulas universitarias. Quizás más lejos, en Israel,
en firme combate contra los árabes. Tal vez más allá, en Irlanda, luchando
fanáticamente por el catolicismo perseguido. Para disimular la sospecha,
ella quita con prolijo gesto la imaginaria arruga del mantel, o arranca
unas hojas secas de los helechos y comienza a hablar, a contarme del
quehacer doméstico, de los vecinos que se están volviendo insoportables,
de que le haría bien a ella entrar al San Juan de Dios de enfermera
voluntaria, porque mi vida aquí, ¿qué es?, pues una sucesión de días sin
sentido, sólo el domingo cambia con la misa y la homilía, después, todo,
bueno, ya sabés, Isidoro, todo es rutinario, aburrido, ¡qué sé yo! ¿No
creés que me haría bien el hospital? Contacto con el dolor, con la
muerte, anticipando su inminente futura llegada. Dos veces por semana,
¿qué pensás, Isidoro?

Afirmo con la cabeza mientras con desánimo compruebo que en las
dos últimas semanas han sido arrestados más de treinta disidentes
políticos en Corea. ¡Pendejos, hasta al poeta Kim Chi Ha lo meten en la
chirona! ¡Grandes carajos que a todo el que se opone al sistema, le
colocan el sanbenito de comunista y a la cárcel se ha dicho . . . ¿De
enfermera voluntaria, verdad? Magnífica idea, pero . . . ¿no decís que
estás muy deprimida y nerviosa sobre todo después de . . . *a-que-llo?*

Cada vez que le recuerdo *aquello*, sus manos tiemblan con un
aletear de pajarillos miedosos, me da la espalda y se va. Después, el
resto del día permanece sumida en un silencio lapidario, con la mirada
fija en el vacío. Me preocupa. Quizás tenga razón y aliviar el dolor de los
otros sea una forma de aliviar el suyo propio. Vive una vida muy suya,
muy metida dentro de ella misma, de la casa, los rutinarios quehaceres,
y claro, con mi trabajo absorbente no le veo solución. Además, es bueno

y saludable ocuparse del prójimo . . . ¿De cuándo acá me nace esta cristianísima preocupación por el prójimo? ¿De cuándo acá creo en los otros y busco su bienestar? Hace ya mucho que me retiré—total deposición de armas—a la más solitaria soledad y ya no hay nada que me saque de mí. Sólo con gestos, con palabras sin sentido me relaciono (me desrelaciono más bien) con los demás. A veces, hasta me sorprendo de que me entiendan; me parece que he dejado de hablar el lenguaje de los otros. Claro, debo de estar cansado, ¡puñeta! Además, tantos años de desilusión . . . y ahora . . . ahora *aquello* que ha ido poniendo distancias entre Nina y yo, me tiene en vilo: en las noches me despierto agitado a observarla. La examino largamente, temiendo que ocurra *aquello* ante mis ojos, pero Nina duerme con tranquilidad; hay un ritmo parejo y acompasado en su respiración. Me pongo entonces a pensar en *aquello* y me preocupo más por Nina. ¡La pobre!, mirá que se necesita estar chiflada para ir por ahí diciendo y clamando *aquello* . . . ¿Que no te he contado *aquello* todavía? ¿Estás seguro, hombre? Mirá que esto sí que se llama despiste mío y de los mayores. Pues nada, viejo, *aquello* (Ella lo denomina así en un sururro lánguido) es ni más ni menos que la súplica repetida que el ánima-en-pena de Paquita Lozano le hace a ella, a Nina, de que revele a la poli la identidad de quien le dio muerte. Nina no conoce a Paquita Lozano. Yo tampoco. Sólo oímos su nombre en las noticias de la tele y fue entonces cuando nos enteramos del crimen. De eso hará un año. Ahora me sale con que se le presenta todas las noches el alma-en-pena de Paquita Lozano y que no encontrará descanso eterno hasta que no prendan a su asesino. El problema es que a Nina le obsesiona la idea de ir a la policía para dar eterno reposo a Paquita Lozano. Por eso he vivido últimamente sin salir ni trabajar, para retenerla, no se me fuera a escapar y entonces, claro, sólo le podría quedar el manicomio. Durante esos días, ella roncaba plácidamente a mi lado, mientras yo no pegaba ojo en toda la noche. Me ponía a leer *La Prensa Libre* y me trasladaba al Japón donde cualquier corporación comercial es una verdadera familia unida como en los tiempos del clan. ¿Quién podría creer que en este vasto mundo cambiante y en un país como el Japón, tan modernizado, se permanezca en una misma firma comercial desde la primera jornada de trabajo hasta el momento del retiro, y que sea tal la identificación del empleado con la compañía, que su desprestigio lo sienta él muy suyo, como pasó con el escándalo Marubeni? ¡Inaudito! ¡Vaya si es inaudito! Hay tantos hechos inauditos en la vida . . . Angustiado, miraba a Nina de nuevo: ella murmuraba algo entre sueños, pero seguía profundamente dormida. ¿Habría inventado *aquello* sólo para llamar mi atención como hacen los niños con los mayores? Con mil asuntos de importancia entre manos, poco a poco me había ido olvidando de ella y la verdad es que la he tenido abandonada por completo. Es obvio, me repetía a mí mismo, Nina quiere inquietarme, tenerme a su merced, saber que a toda hora voy a estar preocupado por ella: esclavo a su entero servicio, eso es lo que quiere.

Además, la poli también me habría tomado por loco como a Nina, y con el puesto que ocupo en el gobierno, esas suposiciones no me habrían favorecido en nada. La amenacé que la encerraría con llave en la despensa si se atrevía a dar un solo paso. Ella alzaba con desdén los hombros, ¡qué putada!, y que nadie la podía detener, porque vos sabés, Isidoro, un alma-en-pena es un alma-en-pena y sólo declarando a la policía el nombre . . . ¿Pero en qué cabeza cabe, mujer de todos los demonios, que así como así se puede acusar a alguien sin prueba alguna?: "Mire usted, señor comisario, a mí se me apareció el ánima-en-pena de Paquita Lozano y me ordenó venir a decirle que el homicida de ella es Juanico Pérez, el mecánico del taller "La Guardia Morada" de Curridabat. Pérez la fue a ver a su apartamento aquella noche pues planeaban ir juntos al cine, pero ya ve usted, señor comisario, a Juanico Pérez se le metió el Cuijen y estranguló a Paquita Lozano en la mismita cama de ella. Eso, eso, señor comisario, la estranguló." "¿Y las pruebas que usted tiene para acusar al interfecto, señor? Muéstreme las pruebas, porque así como así, ¡nada, ni pensarlo! Señora, no se puede acusar a nadie sin pruebas, y menos de semejante delito." A ver, Nina. ¿Qué prueba tenés? Porque todo eso te dirán en la policía, me lo sé, por algo trabajo con el gobierno.

Lo mejor era tratar de conciliar el sueño leyendo, leyendo y leyendo para escapar de *aquello* aunque fuera a medias, porque también las páginas del periódico son una pesadilla plagada de violencia, crímenes, terrorismo, raptos, rehenes, atentados políticos, ataques, masacres, genocidios, guerrillas, ¡qué sé yo! El periódico se me deshace siempre en las manos, empapado de sangre. Además, Nina es zafia, sabe lo que hace y yo tengo que defender de ella mi territorio, no permitir que ella me ocupe por entero, aunque . . . ¿es zafia o . . . estará de veras loca? Tiene una mirada singular, como miraba su madre por aquellos días, cuando asesinó al padre en un arranque de locura. ¡Qué güevonada!, era una mujer suave, mansa, cálida, de manos fláccidas sobre el regazo— como en un interminable reposo—y ojos llenos de distancias y vacíos. Pero un día se hinchó de furor y mató al marido con el cuchillo de cocina. Quién quita que lo haya confundido con un tierno lomito de res. Nina presenció el crimen desde un rincón, ¡la pobre! ¿Hay algo de extraño que después ella también se vuelva loca? A veces, recordando el crimen, me dice con agonía que en los sueños de la noche, vos sabés, Isidoro, yo adivino que dentro de mí va cuajando algo en forma que no alcanzo a distinguir. Es como si todavía la distancia entre eso y yo fuera tal, que su imagen resulta imprecisa. A veces un pedazo de ese algo se aclara, pero como pasa con los rompecabezas complicados, después de juntar una pieza con otra, sólo veo una mancha negra, tal vez un esbozo de retina o la sombra de una nube del diseño total.

¿Y si ese algo impreciso fuera el crimen que a Nina también le crece por dentro? Un día... bueno, pues yo seré la víctima... ¿quién sino yo? Suele dormir muy tranquila a mi lado. ¿Soñará con el otro crimen? El de Paquita Lozano? ¿O con el de su madre?

Cada noche, cada sueño, una pieza más de rompecabezas. Ya no me quedaba duda de que la obsesión suya era el ánima-en-pena de Paquita Lozano: como me negué a ir a la poli, entonces la Lozano se emperró en que teníamos que declarar que había pruebas, y eran unas joyas que el tipo Pérez le había robado la mismita noche del crimen: una madreperla más grande que un guisante, engarzada en sortija de oro muy barroca, y un collar rematado en cruz, también de oro, el Juanico Pérez se los había regalado para Navidad a su amante, Flor María Delgado, del Barrio Amón... Vos sabés que Nina tiene memoria de chorlito. Sin embargo se grabó en su mente dirección exacta y teléfono de la tal Delgado y los repetía como una tarabilla. A partir de ese instante, la inquietud suya ha sido tanta, que ni se cuida de la casa ni de las comidas: que haga lo que quiera la sirvienta, cosa inconcebible en Nina. Además, se pasea de un lado a otro como alma-en-pena y habla sólo para repetir que es inminente presentarse a la poli por el descanso del ánima, de Paquita Lozano: que es nuestro deber. Y lo peor de todo es que... Vos no lo vas a creer, pero igual, debo contártelo. No me mirés así, pues no me estoy volviendo loco. Nina tampoco, ¡ni pensarlo! Es sólo que ella ha cambiado el timbre de voz, suena como si otra persona hablara desde el fondo de su cuerpo. Y también agarró un marcado sonsonete guanacasteco, tragándose las eses y todo. ¿No decían que Paquita Lozano era del Guanacaste? No me mirés así, que no son chifladuras mías. Sólo cuento lo que ha estado ocurriendo. Insólito, pero ya ves, la realidad tiene vainas inexplicables.

Bueno, pues cansado de tanta pendejada—esto debe terminar pronto, tengo que incorporarme al trabajo y Nina, con los antecedentes hereditarios, no puede continuar así—, llamo al teléfono aquel y sí, me contesta la tal Flor de María Delgado. Me hago pasar después por inspector de la Contraloría General de la República y encuentro a la Delgado en la mera dirección luciendo tamaña madreperla engarzada en oro barroco. Que si conoce a Juanico Pérez, le repito, porque ella está turbada y mientras busca la respuesta, se hace la que no me oye.

El encuentro con Flor de María Delgado fue para mí como si *aquello*—el rompecabezas sin resolver—estuviera en un tris de quedar completo. ¿Cómo sabía Nina de la Delgado y su amante y la madreperla y todo eso? Ah, se me olvidaba contarte, viejo, que la descripción que Nina hizo de ella, no podía ser más exacta. Ni que la conociera a las mil maravillas. Hasta el detalle de la risa estrepitosa y del mechón de pelo oxigenado que le cae tapándole el ojo derecho y que ella retira mecánicamente con displicencia. Yo, que entonces estaba embebido en las persecuciones, torturas y control represivo de los atroces gobiernos totalitarios en Latinoamérica; y que había comenzado a sumirme en la vida miserable del Charles Chaplin huérfano que paseaba su hambre por

125

las calles de Londres y que después, rico, se dedicaba a denunciar los males de nuestra sociedad, perdí interés en el genial cómico, abandoné libros, revistas, periódicos, todo, porque ¡qué carajo!, hay que hacer algo por Paquita Lozano para darle descanso a su ánima-en-pena y dejar de penar nosotros dos. Vos lo ves, me ha costado venir, pero aquí me tenés, y que Juanico Pérez me perdone. ¿Me lo creés todo? ¿Verdad que me lo creés todo? Te repito, pensé al principio que eran chifladuras de mi mujer y que estaba a un paso del manicomio. Ustedes buscan al asesino y nosotros, que no lo conocemos, que tampoco conocimos a su víctima, traemos el rompecabezas, digo, el crimen, resuelto, cuando ustedes lo daban por indescifrable. ¿Verdad que me creés y van a prender a Juanico Pérez? Por lo visto eso de un ánima-en-pena es algo serio e impostergable. Ah, no, no me mirés así, viejo . . .

Roberta Fernández

Zulema

yo ya enterré a tus muertos
bajo un trigal al viento

Lucha Corpi

I

Lo que oyó Zulema aquella mañana en 1914 le cambió la vida y desde ese año se tuvo que enfrentar a las consecuencias de loa que había escuchado aquel romoto martes otoñal. Durante toda la noche anterior había escuchado los tiroteos esporádicos de los Federales luchando con los Villistas. El ruido y la cama poco conocida la despertaron mucho antes de que el repique de las campanas de San Agustín diera su llamada cotidiana a los parroquianos. A las seis de la mañana cuando los primeros sonidos del campanario resonaban a la distancia, Zulema se levantó e inmediatamente se hincó a decir sus rezos matinales. Oyó a Mariana en el cuarto de al lado y pensó que los disturbios de la noche también la habían levantado un poco más temprano de lo que acostumbraba.

Mariana se veía diferente esta mañana, con los ojos hinchados y algo tensa mientras preparaba el café y las tortillas de harina. Zulema creyó que había interrumpido a su tía al entrar a la cocina a pesar de que Mariana instintivamente había dejado el comal para saludar a la niña con un beso. "Te tengo muchas noticias," Mariana había susurrado a la vez que abrazaba el cuerpecito de Zulema. Y así fue como Mariana le contó la historia.

La voz le salía un poco falsa y era obvio que trataba de mantener una cara limpia de emoción. Pero no dejaba de dar impresión de gran cansancio. Después, cuando Zulema trataba de recordar la escena, lo único que podía captar era la palidez de Mariana y su voz temblorosa. En este tono Mariana le había dicho que su nuevo hermano por fin había llegado durante la noche, cansado de su viaje pero contento, gordito y lleno de vida.

La noche había estado repleta de actividad, Mariana continuó diciéndole. Además de los tiroteos al otro lado, también había venido un mensajero desde San Antonio pidiendo que Isabel se fuera a cuidar a Carmen, quien sufría de una pulmonía muy grave. Isabel se había ido en seguida con el mensajero, dejando al recién nacido con el resto de la familia. Tan pronto que se mejorara Carmen, ella regresaría a casa. Dale

127

a mi Zulemita y a mi Miguelito un beso y diles que pronto volveré.
Según Mariana ésas habían sido las últimas palabras de su hermana
Isabel.

"Tú te quedarás conmigo por un rato," le dijo a Zulema. Miguel se
quedaría con su padre y la abuela, y el recién nacido se iría con Doña
Julia quien vivía a cruzar la calle. Ella también tenía una criaturita a
quien todavía estaba amamantando. Tal como lo presentaba Mariana
todo había quedado arreglado.

II

Pasaron treinta y cinco años. Luego, sentada en el suelo de la
recámara de Zulema, respaldada contra unos almohadones que me había
hecho, yo oía muchas versiones de lo que años después reconocería
como la misma historia. Durante aquellas visitas escuchaba la voz profunda y
serena de Zulema con la que me contaba un cuento tras otro. Llenaba el
cuarto de personajes fantásticos con eccentricidades muy peculiares
quienes seguían girando en mi propia imaginación acelerada. Muchos
de sus cuentos eran simplemente versiones de los que había oído de
Mariana pero la mayoría de sus narraciones las había inventado ella
misma. De tarde en tarde Mariana nos acompañaba, silenciosa en su
mecedora y con los ojos cerrados.

Mariana a veces abría los ojos, se apoyaba en el brazo de la mecedora
para escuchar mejor y luego movía la cabeza de lado a lado para corregir
a Zulema. "No, no fue así." Y se dirigía hacia mí con su propia versión
del cuento que acabábamos de oír. Me solía ser difícil decidir cuál de
las narraciones me gustaba más porque cada una tenía su toque con la
descripción y sabía exactamente dónde pausar para el máximo efecto,
pero supongo que en ese entonces creía que la "bola de años" de
Mariana—tal como se refería a su edad—le daba una ventaja sobre
Zulema.

Poco a poco me fui dando cuenta de que Zulema tenía un cuento
favorito, el de la soldadera Victoriana quien a la cumbre de la revolución
se había venido a este lado a esperar a su novio Joaquín. Por un tiempo la
gente que venía de su pueblo en Zacatecas le confirmaba su fe en que
Joaquín todavía estaba vivo pero al pasar los años, todo mundo simplemente
se fue olvidando de Victoriana. Ella continuó vigilando hasta aquella
tarde inesperada cuando, después de treinta años, la gente la encontró
sentada en la misma silla en donde había iniciado su espera, cubierta de
telarañas y polvo rojizo, con su rifle mohoso a sus pies y una expresión
resplandeciente en la cara.

Nunca me cansaba del cuento de Zulema puesto que cada vez que
me lo recitaba hacía como si fuera la primera vez que me contaba de
Victoriana y ella retocaba los hechos con unos que otros detalles más. El
clímax, sin embargo, era siempre el mismo y me describía como Victoriana no había podido reconocer al hombre cuya memoria había

amado durante todos esos años, pues cuando los periódicos habían publicado la historia de Victoriana, Joaquín había venido a verla de pura curiosidad. Y resultó que ella no lo había separado de todos los demás visitantes a quienes había saludado esa tarde. Él, ya no siendo el campesino con quien ella se había enamorado sino un negociante bastante conocido, se había divertido y avergonzado a la vez por todos los mosquitos y las mariposas que ella llevaba en las telarañas que cubrían, como una patina, su melena bien plateada.

Zulema concluía el cuento: Victoriana abordaba los Ferrocarriles Nacionales Mexicanos y los fronterizos se despedían tristemente de la figura espléndida y extravagante que había roto la rutina de sus vidas por un instante. Victoriania hacía ondular un pañuelo blanco al ritmo del movimiento del tren que la llevaba a su pueblo donde pensaba localizar a los parientes quienes había visto por última vez en Bachimba, reclamando sus rifles y cabalgando hacia la distancia antes de que la fuerza de la revolución les controlara el destino.

Finales desconocidos, vidas inconcluídas. Esos eran los temas de casi todos los cuentos de Zulema aunque yo no podría decir cuándo comencé a darme cuenta de esto. El día en que cumplí seis años sentí que algo había cambiado puesto que Zulema pasó de la fantasía a la biografía y por primera vez me mencionó a Isabel. Sacó una fotografía desde su misal y me la mostró. "¿Sabes quién es?"

De inmediato reconocí la foto como una copia de una que tenía mi madre. "Es tu mamá," le respondí en seguida. "Mi abuelita Isabel."

Cuántas veces no había abierto y cerrado el primer cajón del armario de mi madre para poder lograr un vistazo de la joven en su blusa de encaje quien me veía con una mirada suave y directa. Jamás me habían hablado acerca de ella. Sólo sabía que era la madre de mi padre quien había muerto al dar a luz a mi tío Luis.

"Murió cuando tenía veinte y cuatro años. Yo tenía seis entonces," Zulema me dijo en una voz quedita. "Mariana de veras me tomó el pelo diciéndome que mamá se había ido con la tía Carmen."

La foto a su pecho, Zulema comenzó a dar un suspiro tras otro y de repente lloraba sin control. A través de las lágrimas me contó como había esperado a su madre todos los días de aquel primer invierno cuando Isabel se había ido sin ninguna despedida. Cuando oía pasar gente por la calle, corría a la puerta a averiguar quién era. El ruido del tranvía que pasaba en frente de la casa la alertaba a la posibilidad de que su madre viniera en él y cada vez que veía a Julia amamantar al bebé, se preguntaba si Luisito no echaba de menos el sabor de su propia madre. Comenzó a sentirse abandonada y a hablar de sus sentimientos. Sin embargo, todos mantenían la historia que Mariana le había contado. ¿Cuándo, cuándo, cuándo va a volver? le preguntaba a la tía y Mariana por fin le había contestado, "Cuando termine la guerra, volverá."

Y así fue que la pequeña Zulema a los ocho años se interesó en la guerra. Por la noche cuando oía los tiros o las ambulancias, sollazaba contra la almohada hasta que se quedaba dormida. Al oír las cornetas militares por la mañana, se quedaba tiesa por unos instantes. En las tardes, después de su clase, se iba caminando cerca del río para poder mirar hacia la nación al otro lado, abrumada por la guerra. Cerraba los ojos y suplicaba con todo su ser que terminara el conflicto y, entonces, siempre veía a su madre acercársele con los brazos extendidos. Zulema sin embargo no podía fiarse de esa imagen porque sabía que la guerra no estaba para terminar. Todos los días se daba cuenta de toda la gente que seguía cruzando el puente con todos sus efectos en carretones o en maletas de todo tipo o hasta en morrales al hombro, cansados y gastados por las angustias personales que ellos también estaban pasando. A veces su padre la daba trabajo en la marqueta o en el rancho a algunos de los recién llegados y entonces Zulema tomaba la oportunidad para hacerles preguntas acerca de la guerra antes de que ellos siguieran más al norte. Nadie tenía la menor idea de cuándo terminaría la revolución y había una que otra persona a quien ya no le importaba lo que pasaba excepto por la manera en que los hechos le estaban cambiando el curso de la vida. Su preocupación principal se enfocaba en la muerte y en la destrucción que tomaba control de todo.

Oyendo tantos episodios en donde la muerte dominaba, Zulema se iba poniendo aprehensiva. Entre más oía a los refugiados, más iba asociando las experiencias de ellos con la pérdida de su madre y lentamente comenzó a dudar la asociación del regreso de Isabel con el final de la guerra.

Un día trató de contarle a Carmela—quien acababa de empezar a trabajar en casa—de su madre y se dió cuenta de que ya no tenía una imagen clara de ella. La memoria misma se comenzaba a hacer memoria y ésta ya se iba borrando en los detalles más inesperados.

Ya para el día de su cumpleaños en 1917 estaba lista para echarles la lanza a todos y cuando los tenía a su alrededor les dijo que sabía que la guerra supuestamente había terminado y sin embargo su madre no había vuelto. "Sé que se perdió," dijo muy deliberadamente y luego, mirando a Mariana, anunció con un tono de finalidad, "Yo ya no tengo mamá."

Y ese mismo día comenzó a contar sus cuentos. Se llevó a Miguelito y a Luisito a su cuarto y los sentó en el suelo; ella se recostó sobre la cama mirando el techo. "Les voy a contar un cuento de nunca acabar," empezó mientras narraba su versión de la Bella Durmiente, a quien la había encantado su madrastra malvada. De este encanto la iba a despertar un beso de un maravilloso príncipe pero eso no pudo suceder. Se dirigió a sus hermanos y les preguntó si sabían por qué el príncipe no había logrado encontrar a la Bella Durmiente. Sin darles la oportunidad de contestar puesto que éste era su propio cuento, ella continuó con gestos melodramáticos.

El príncipe no pudo encontrar a la Bella Durmiente decía en voz baja, porque cuando él apenas empezaba su búsqueda, estalló una revolución y le llegó la noticia de que Emiliano Zapata le iba a confiscar su caballo blanco. Así es que el príncipe tuvo que irse a pie y como no estaba acostumbrado a valerse por sí mismo, no tenía ninguna idea de cómo llegar a su destinación. Decidió regresar a su castillo pero cuando se acercaba a él, vio que los revolucionarios lo habían volado a cañonazos. Ellos habían declarado también que él ya no podía ser un príncipe sino que ahora era una persona como todas las demás. Así que no pudo lograr su misión y la pobre Bella Durmiente se quedó allá en el bosque totalmente olvidada. Llegó el día en que nadie se acordaba, ni mucho menos se preocupaba de los problemas de aquella pobrecita Bella Durmiente tan tonta que había pensado que necesitaba vivir en un castillo con un príncipe. Así es que sin darse cuenta de las repercusiones de sus hechos, los revolucionarios habían logrado deshacerse de todos los príncipes igual que de todas las mimadas Bellas Durmientes.

Me pasé aquella tarde escuchando a Zulema recitar cuentos de esta índole uno tras otro, interrumpidos por lágrimas y frecuentes lapsos en el silencio. Desde que era niña, me decía, a sus hermanos no les gustaban sus tramas porque los consideraban extrañas. A veces hasta encontraban sus finales mórbidos. De vez en cuando había tratado de contarle sus cuentos a su padre pero él no tenía el menor interés en ellos. Mariana, quien tal vez mejor entendía lo que ella trataba de decir, pensaba que tenía derecho de cambiarle sus finales. Por eso Zulema había sentido la falta de audiencia y se había tenido que tragar sus cuentos durante todos esos años. Yo era la única que la había dejado contarlos exactamente como los quería decir.

"Zulema, a mí me gustan tus cuentos," yo le aseguraba, deshaciéndole las trenzas para luego peinarla con mis pequeños dedos.

La miraba a través de mis propias lágrimas. Zulema no se parecía a Mariana ni a la Isabel de la foto. Ella solía verse bastante ordinaria, con su pelo apartado por el centro y plegado en dos trenzas gruesas que sobrecruzaba en estilo tradicional al frente de la cabeza. No se parecía a mi madre tampoco quien lucía el estilo del día con su cabello peinado hacia atrás cubriendo una rata postiza que llevaba prendida al margen del cráneo. A mí me gustaba más el cabello de Zulema y me encantaba desentrenzarlo y luego cepillarlo hasta que le sacaba todas las ondas, haciéndolo llegar hasta su cintura.

Esa tarde le presté una atención muy especial y le entrencé un listón rojo de satín que la hacía más linda. Durante el rato en que yo le hacía sus toquecitos de belleza, ella continuaba con la narrativa que no había compartido por tantos años. Se olvidó de la elaboración que solía darle a sus otros cuentos y al describir el acontecimiento principal de su vida fue directa y tersa. No culpaba a Mariana ni a su padre ya que ellos obviamente habían esperado protegerla del mismo dolor que le habían causado. Poco a poco, me decía, se le fue acabando la esperanza de poder ver a su madre de nuevo y para los doce años dejó de creer en su regreso. Sin embargo, a veces al abrir alguna puerta en casa de su padre, tenía la sensación de que Isabel estaba sentada en su sillón. Otras veces, sólo por un instante, veía a una figura luminosa con un niño en los brazos pero no lograba verles la cara por el brillo que irradiaba de ellos. Más o menos por esos días fue cuando comenzó a abrir de par en par todas las puertas en casa. Se fue fascinando también con los baúles y las cajas que estaban guardadas en el sótano.

Un día cuando visitaba a su padre y a Amanda, Zulema se halló sola en el despacho del padre. Comenzó a esculcar en el escritorio y de repente en uno de los cajones, debajo de algunas fotos y álbumes, encontró lo que había andado buscando sin darse cuenta durante todos esos meses. Allí estaba una esquela con sus márgenes negros y letras embozadas. La agarró y leyó: *ISABEL MENDOZA CARDENAS, esposa de José María del Valle—1890-1914.* Leyó las palabras muchas veces sin emoción. Luego siguió con el resto del anuncio. Éste indicaba que ella había sido sobrevivida por tres hijos, Zulema, Miguel y Luis.

Zulema dejó la esquela en el mismo sitio, tal como la había encontrado. Después de esa tarde dejó de abrir puertas y cajas, aún hasta en casa de Mariana. Comenzó a levantarse a las seis de la mañana para poder asistir a misa en San Agustín donde se quedaba hasta las ocho y media cuando tenía que irse a la escuela. Sin darse cuenta, fue perdiendo interés en lo que pasaba en sus clases y un jueves decidió quedarse en la iglesia todo el día. Por varias semanas se sentó en la inmensa iglesia donde el incienso le suavizaba las memorias y las velas que iba encendiendo le aclaraban la oscuridad. El Padre Salinas comenzó a notar que las velas iban despareciendo y que sus parroquianos no estaban dejando suficiente dinero para cubrir el costo. Al siguiente día encontró a Zulema sentada en la primera fila viendo a la Virgen con el niño Jesús. Luego la vio prender unas dos o tres velas a la vez, y cuando éstas se acababan en sus veleros verdes, observaba que encendía otras más.

Casi al mismo tiempo que el Padre Salinas le hablaba a Mariana de los gastos eclesiásticos, la maestra visitó a José María. Él ni discutió el asunto con su hija sino que habló directamente con la cuñada. Mariana entonces le dijo a Zulema que su padre quería que ella se quedara en casa puesto que ya no podián fiarse de ella. De hoy en adelante tendría que ser acompañada o por uno de los primos o una de las tías.

A Zulema en realidad no le preocuparon las restricciones ya que jamás se había sentido el objeto de tanta atención. Mariana comenzó a enseñarle como hacer platos tradicionales. Para el mole necesitaban pasarse buena parte de un día moliendo las semillas de ajonjolí en el metate igual que las semillas de cacao y los cacahuates. Mientras preparaban los ingredientes para la salsa y antes de empezar a cocinarla, salían al gallinero a escoger dos o tres pollos bien gordos. Zulema aprendió pronto a torcer el pescuezo del pollo antes de cortarle la cabeza con un machetazo bien dado. Le encantaba preparar la capirotada y la leche quemada para el postre y la primera vez que preparó toda una cena para doce personas gozó de todos los cumplidos que recibió, especialmente por su riquísima fritada de cabrito.

Doña Julia le enseñó a tejer blusas y guantes con gancho lo mismo que manteles y sobrecamas que hacía para regalos de primera comunión, de fiestas de quinceañeras y de boda. Cuando ella cumplió los quince años fue festejada con un baile al cual asistieron todos los parientes, sus amigos y los amigos de su padre, quienes bailaron a la música de un combo local con la feliz festejada hasta la madrugada.

Esa fue la primera vez que conoció a Carlos con quien bailó muchas veces durante el transcurso de la noche. Pocos días después, él fue a pedirle permiso a José María para visitar a Zulema en casa. Sus amigas comenzaron a molestarla con bromas de la edad acerca de novios. Hasta las amigas de Mariana que se reunían de vez en cuando a coser sus colchas le comenzaron a preguntar acerca de Carlos. Zulema se sonreía tímidamente mientras se hacía concentrar en las puntadas. Su primera colcha fue de felpa blanca por un lado y de satín por el otro. Ésta se la regaló a su prima Elena cuando nació su tercer hijo. Después de unos meses comenzó a llenar su propio baúl con sus obras y cuando se casó con Carlos llevó a su casa todo lo necesario para empezar una vida nueva.

Tan pronto como tuvieron su primer hijo, Mariana se vino a vivir con ellos y por más de veinte años los tres habían visto a la familia crecer y luego empequeñecerse de nuevo cuando los hijos mayores se habían ido a estudiar a Austin y la hija menor se había casado, como su madre, a los diez y siete años.

Zulema había tratado de envolver a cada uno de sus hijos en sus cuentos pero a los cuatro les habían parecido tontos y repetitivos. Así que no fue hasta que yo comencé a hacerle pedidos diarios de sus recitaciones que ella comenzó a considerar las razones de los varios huecos en su vida.

"Es lo que más me ha gustado—contar cuentos," me decía. Se había calmado durante el transcurso de la tarde que ya había entrado en estado crepuscular.

"A mí también," me sonreí mientras le estiraba los listones rojos.

En ese momento se abrió la puerta y mi prima Marcia prendió la luz. "¿Qué están haciendo ustedes dos sentadas en la oscuridad? Ay, mamá, te ves tan chistosa con esos listones."

"No es cierto," la contradije. "Se ve muy linda."

Marica echó mi comentario al lado con un movimiento de la mano. "Ustedes dos, siempre con sus juegos de fantasía. Vénganse. Traje una charola de pollo frito y ensalada de papa. Ahora mismo voy a poner la mesa. ¿Vienen a cenar con nosotros?"

"Horita vamos," le contestó Zulema. "Déjanos terminar aquí."

En el instante en que quedamos solas, Zulema me miró fijamente.

"Vamos a guardar todo esto en secreto. Pobre Mariana. Hace tanto tiempo que murió mamá. Ya ni para qué andar haciendo borloteos."

III

Por la cuarta vez releí lo que había escrito para el día 16 de abril. Cambié unas cuantas palabras, luego cerré el cuaderno, frotando la lisura de la cubierta de cuera y recordando lo feliz que había estado cuando Mariana y Zulema me regalaron el cuaderno la Navidad pasada.

Esta tarde el sol brillaba muy fuerte y como, en la prisa para salir a la estación de camiones, me olvidé mis lentes oscuros, tuve que cerrar los ojos contra el deslumbramiento de la tarde y traté de dormirme. Después de unos minutos abrí los ojos de nuevo, esta vez para averiguar la hora. Todavía nos faltaban dos horas y media para llegar. Del asiento vacío a mi lado tomé la revista que había comprado en la tienda del Greyhound en San Antonio y las hojeé. Noticias de Cuba, Viet Nam y Laos. Una foto sonriente de Barbra Streisand y otra chistosa de los Beatles.

Me recargué contra la ventana y extendí las piernas sobre los dos asientos. Desde esa posición podía ver a los otros pasajeros. La mujer que iba dos filas hacia mi izquierda me recordaba a la madre de Florinda con su pelo bien rastrillado. Volví a cerrar los ojos.

Todavía no había conocido a la madre de Florinda pero por lo que me había contado mi hermana, tenía una idea muy clara de cómo se veía el día en que había abandonado Cuba hacía cinco años. Durante el año que había preparado la salida se había dejado crecer el pelo lo más que pudo. Y el día en que salieron se hizo un peinado muy extravagante al estilo moño francés. La parte que quedaba cubierta la había divido en tres secciones. Primero se había hecho un moño pequeñito que había sostenido con unas horquillas encrustadas de joyas, una verdadera fortuna me habían dicho. Este pequeño moño fue cubierto por otro más grande, también sostenido por más horquillas con joyas. La capa de encima fácilmente cubría las joyas pero el escondite iba todavía más protegido por una capa de laca bien dura. Casi como para burlarse del destino se había decorado el peinado con mariposas de gaza blanca y color de rosa que iban atadas al cabello con unos alambritos muy finitos.

Según Florinda su madre se veía tan ridícula que nadie la había tomado en cuenta y por eso logró hacer el papel de contrabandista. Con lo que había sacado, la familia estableció una pequeña tienda de telas que, cuatro años más tarde, ya tenía bastante éxito.

Abrí los ojos para ver a la señora a mi izquierda. "Coño," pensé al encender un cigarrillo. Debido al ángulo con el que me pegaba el sol, el humo del cigarrillo parecía hacer espirales de niebla tupida. Me quedé viendo esas vueltas de humo que ondulaban como los vapores tumultuosos que le dificultaban la búsqueda de su padre a Juan Preciado en la película que acababa de ver la semana pasada. En realidad la obra de

Rulfo tenía mucho que ver con este viaje que estaba haciendo ahora mismo.

"Ésta es mi novela favorita," les había asegurado a Zulema y a Mariana, "aunque hay mucho en ella que sé que no entiendo muy bien," y con esto las había presentado a los espíritus de Comala durante mis vacaciones de Thanksgiving. Por tres días estuvimos leyendo de las copias de *Pedro Páramo* que les había traído de regalo. Mariana y yo hacíamos la lectura en voz alta y de vez en cuando Zulema también tomaba su turno. Mientras comentábamos la lectura, Mariana había sacado su botella de Chivas Regal y entre sorbitos de whiskey tratábamos de sacarle sentido a los pasajes más intrigantes. A Mariana, en particular, le gustaban los personajes del Rancho Media Luna ya que ellos formaban parte de un período que ella todavía recordaba bien. Y Zulema, tal como había anticipado yo, se había identificado con el personaje de Dolores cuyo destino también había sido afectado por la muerte prematura de su madre.

"Los espíritus siempre siguen afectando a los que les sobreviven," Mariana lamentó. "Aquí mismo tenemos el ejemplo de Zulema, quien sufrió tanto después de la muerte de Isabel."

Zulema y yo nos vimos una a la otra. Después de cincuenta años de la muerte de su hermana, Mariana había decidido romper el silencio.

"¿Por qué dices eso, Mariana?" le pregunté casi en susorro.

"Es que los murmullos se ponen más fuertes cada día," ella había contestado, extendiendo las manos sobre la silla. Cerró los ojos y comenzó a moverse en la mecedora con determinación. La conversación había terminado; por lo menos no quería más preguntas. Después de unos cuantos segundos se paró y nos dio una mirada intensa a la vez que murmuraba, "Ya es tiempo." Y dijo que nos iba a llevar a la tumba de Isabel.

En rumbo al cementerio llevamos un silencio abrumador. Yo me hacía pregunta tras pregunta. Como el resto de la familia yo también había sucumbido casi totalmente a la historia de la partida de Isabel y ni había preguntado jamás dónde estaba sepultada. Por quince años, desde el día en que Zulema me había contado su versión de la muerte de su madre, yo había separado a Isabel del mundo corporal y la había colocado en el reino de los espíritus. No me podía imaginar lo conmovida que debería estar Zulema. Ella no había dicho ninguna palabra desde el instante en que Mariana mencionó a Isabel.

"Vamos por este camino," Mariana nos señalaba la parte vieja del cementerio, por donde nos llevaba, hasta que llegamos al lado de una tumba con un ramillete de caléndulas en un bote rojo de lata. Ésta estaba medio enterrado al frente de la piedra sepulcrar que conmemoraba la vida y la muerte de "Isabel Mendoza Cárdenas, quien nació en 1890 y murió en 1914."

Me acerqué a Zulema y vi que le temblaban los labios. Luego

135

comenzó a hacer gemidos. Mariana también se le arrimó para abrazarla. Luego apoyó la cabeza contra el hombro de Zulema.

"Yo nunca supe cómo remediar lo que pasó," dijo sencillamente. Era obvio que quería contarnos lo que había pasado y, como le dolían las piernas, caminamos unos metros a una sillita blanca de hierro forjado. Las tres nos mantuvimos en silencio por un rato. Por fin Mariana comenzó a contarnos del dilema que había pasado cuando la familia la había escogido para transmitirle a Zulema la historia que habían inventado de la muerte de Isabel. Desde el principio había hecho ajustes cuando en lugar de asistir a la novena para su hermana se había quedado en casa con Zulema. Y cuando la niña había comenzado a mostrar su desconfianza, ella había empezado a dudar la decisión de protegerla de la realidad.

Pero después de un tiempo, decía Mariana, ellas mismas casi habían aceptado la historia como verdad y tácitamente creían que sería mucho más difícil ajustarse a una nueva realidad que seguir con lo que ya estaba en desarrollo. "No sabía qué hacer," Mariana nos seguía repitiendo.

También nos contó de sus visitas semanales al cementerio que le ayudaban a mantener viva la memoria de Isabel. Por años se había salido a las escondidas para venir en camión con su ramillete de tres caléndulas que ponía en un boto limpio de Folger's. Al pasar los años sus visitas se hacían más esporádicas. Sin embargo, la semana pasada había traído el pequeño ramillete que acabamos de ver.

Señalándole a Mariana sus piernas reumáticas, le preguntaba como había podido mantener durante tantos años la manera que había escogido para honrar a su hermana.

"No ves que si uno tiene la posibilidad de escoger entonces simplemente uno actúa de acuerdo con lo que sabe que se tiene que hacer. Es todo," afirmó.

Durante el resto del día yo trataba de juntar todas las diferentes partes de la historia para sacarles sentido. En unas páginas sueltas comencé a escribir trozos largos acerca de Mariana, Isabel y Zulema. Al volver a mi cuarto en el dormitorio seguí con lo que había empezado y un día en la primera semana de diciembre metí todas mis notas en un sobre y se las envié a Mariana y a Zulema con instrucciones de que me guardaran las páginas. El resultado de estas notas fue mi diario encuadernado en cuero, color borgoña.

Lo busqué en el asiento a mi lado y al tocarlo abrí los ojos. Acabábamos de llegar. Mientras el camión cruzaba las calles en rumbo a la terminal, yo cogí mis maletines y me fuí acercando a la puerta. Tan pronto llegamos a la terminal, vi a Patricia en su pequeño Volkswagen.

"Espero no llegar tarde. ¿Está viva todavía?" le pregunté a mi hermana al abrir la puerta del carro.

"Pues se ha estado manteniendo con un hilito pero no creo que va a durar mucho más," me contestó al arrancarse hacia el hospital. "Esta mañana tuvo otro ataque de corazón y el médico no piensa que va a sobrevivirlo."

IV

Sentí el olor del incienso y el murmullo de rezos tan pronto que abrí la puerta del cuarto 306. El Padre Murphy echaba el agua bendita y recitaba los versos del último sacramento sobre el cuerpo en el lecho. Mi madre me tomó la mano y dijo muy quedito, "Murió hace unos quince minutos."

Sentía que todo mundo me veía mientras caminaba hacia el lecho. Me agaché para besar las mejillas bien lisas y por largo rato miré al cuerpo sin decir nada. Y de repente me di cuenta de lo que tenía que hacer.

Me fui en el carro de mi hermana al otro lado del río a la iglesia por la primera plaza donde muchas veces había visto las ofrendas de milagros prendidos con alfileres a la ropa de los santos. En la tienda de artículos religiosos que estaba al lado de la iglesia encontré en venta muchísimos milagros que venían en diferentes tamaños, formas y materiales. Los grandes no me interesaban y sabía que no podía comprar los de oro. Así es que de los milagros de lata de media pulgada escogí cuidadosamente los que venían en formas de perfiles humanos, corazones ardientes y lenguas alumbradas. La voluntaria de la tienda se sorprendió cuando le dije que quería cinco docenas de cada uno pero después de su reacción inicial esperó con paciencia mientras que yo hacía mi selección y fue poniendo los milagros en tres bolsitas de plástico.

Volví al carro y me dirigí al mercado de flores donde escogí varias docenas de caléndulas. Les pedí que me las dividieran en ramilletes de tres flores y las amarraran con listoncitos blancos. Las flores casi llenaron el asiento de atrás y el inspector de la aduana comentó sobre mi ofrenda de fores "para los muertos." Al volver a este lado me paré en una papelería donde compré velas coloradas perfumadas de canela. Ya en rumbo a Brewster Funeral Parlor donde pensaba dejar mis compras por unas horas, pasé en frente de una "discolandia." Pronto puse los frenos, me estacioné al lado y entré corriendo a preguntar si tenían unos discos, en blanco, tamaño 45. El dependiente me dijo que tenían tres tales discos de una orden especial que ya tenía mucho tiempo en la tienda. Después de que él los encontró, volví al carro.

Por fin llegué a las funerarias donde le tuve que explicar al administrador lo que proponía hacer. El por fin me dio permiso de llevar a cabo mis planes pero solamente después de que le había explicado todos los detalles por lo menos cinco veces.

A la hora en que habíamos quedado de acuerdo volví a las funerarias y por tres o cuatro horas me dediqué a mi labor. Sabía que después de medianoche el cadáver estaría listo para ser vigilado por familia y amigos. Me dolía la espalda de estar doblada por tanto tiempo pero continué cosiendo los milagros en el satín que cubría el interior del ataúd. Con tres pespuntes apretados pasaba el ojito de cada figura de lata para hacer tres arcos en el satín—las caritas quedaban en la fila de afuera, las lenguas quedaban por en medio y los corazones formaban la fila de adentro. Cuando terminé con los milagros, di unos pasos hacia atrás para mirarlos desde otra perspectiva. Me parecían hermosos, cada uno con su pequeñito listoncito rojo. Imaginaba como, una vez cerrado el ataúd, desde adentro se lograría esta magnífica belleza colorida.

Luego arreglé las caléndulas en una auréola alrededor del cadáver. Las velas las puse en una fila en frente del ataúd con el propósito de que sus olores rompieran los confines del espacio. Finalmente puse los tres discos al lado izquierdo del cadáver. "Llénalos con tus cuentos favoritos," le murmuré, tocándole la cara.

Una vez terminado mi labor me quedé sentada en la semi-oscuridad dejándome llevar por el mesmerismo del olor de las flores y el resplandor perfumado de las velas.

Por fin me levanté y caminé hacia el ataúd. Los milagros se veían espléndidos pero de todos modos no sabía cuál sería la reacción por parte de la familia. Me quedé viendo a la figura tan querida por última vez y luego salí de la funeraria, sabiendo que no iría al entierro al día siguiente.

Tan pronto como llegué a casa comencé a escribir en mi cuaderno color borgoña. Por dos días estuve escribiendo hasta que llené todas las páginas. Luego le pasé el libro a Patricia pidiéndole que leyera lo que acababa de terminar.

Empezó en la primera página y leyó por varias horas. A veces veía que movía la cabeza de lado a lado y casi hacía sonidos para sí misma. Cuando terminó, cerró el libro pero dejó una mano sobre él.

"No," me dijo. "No fue así." Mientras hablaba le cruzó por la cara una expresión de desaprueba. "Esto no ha sido de ninguna manera como lo has presentado. Has hecho una mezcolanza de algunos de los cuentos que te contaron Mariana y Zulema, que en primer lugar tal vez ni eran ciertos. Yo he oído otras versiones de la Tía Carmen y aún de Zulema. No creo que Mariana jamás se reconocería si le enseñaras lo que tienes aquí."

"Pues yo no entiendo lo que estás tratando de decir," continuó Patricia, "pero protesto porque lo que tienes aquí no es lo que pasó."

Luz María Umpierre

La Ansiedad de la Influencia en Sandra María Esteves y Marjorie Agosin

Los estudios que toman como objeto de investigación las obras de los escritores hispanos en los Estados Unidos han seguido hasta el presente aproximaciones críticas temáticas o socio-históricas. Estas aproximaciones han sido necesarias para sentar la base desde la cual ir revelando, descubriendo, aquello que une a estos escritores entre sí y el impulso inicial que genera sus textos. Dentro de esos estudios fundamentales, es necesario señalar dos de ellos por el nuevo camino que sugieren a la crítica.

Margarita Fernández Olmos en "From The Metropolis: Puerto Rican Women Poets and the Immigration Experience" señala cómo la escritora latina en los Estados Unidos tiene la difícil tarea de defender la cultura de la cual se encuentra deprivada a la vez que analiza con ojo crítico esa misma cultura de la que es víctima.[1] Aunque el planteamiento de Fernández Olmos se hace en referencia a la mujer puertorriqueña, la distinción que hace es válida al definir la problemática de la escritora chicana, en particular, y es extensible a la escritora hispana en los Estados Unidos en general.[2] De gran interés es la aseveración de Fernández Olmos de que la poesía escrita por puertorriqueñas está evolucionando no sólo temática sino estéticamente.

Por otro lado, capital en el estudio de la poesía hispana en los Estados Unidos es el prológo de Efraín Barradas a la muestra de poesía puertorriqueña en los Estados Unidos titulado *Herejes y mitificadores*.[3] En este estudio, Barradas distingue dos movimientos temáticos dentro de la literatura escrita por puertorriqueños en los Estados Unidos. Ello lo hace en base a la aceptación o rechazo que la poesía de estos escritores hace de los mitos que sostienen la cultura puertorriqueña: ". . . nuestros poetas, que miran la cultura puertorriqueña desde afuera, son herejes o mitificadores con relación a varios mitos donde creen encontrar encarnada la esencia de la puertorriqueñidad."[4] Al igual que en el caso de Fernández Olmos, nos atrevemos a decir que esa disyuntiva es la misma que existe en las obras de otros grupos hispanos en este país, según se acercan o se separan de sus respectivas culturas de origen.

El señalamiento de Fernández Olmos de un cambio estético nos ha llevado a emprender una nueva lectura de las obras de dos escritoras hispanas residentes en los Estados Unidos: Sandra María Esteves (puertorriqueña) y Marjorie Agosin (chilena). El carácter metapoético presente en algunos de los poemas de estas escritoras nos lleva a sugerir que la clasificación temática de Barradas podría ser ampliada para incluir un movimiento de revisión en una de estas escritoras, y otro de descontinuidad en la otra. En los dos poemas que utilizaremos como modelos para nuestro estudio, la hablante en cada uno de ellos se dirige a poetas conocidos en el ámbito literario de los países de origen de las escritoras. Nuestro análisis se facilitará teniendo en cuenta las teorías de Harold Bloom.[5] La selección crítica se debe a que es innegable el hecho de que ambas poetas, al dirigirse a estas figuras representativas de la tradición literaria de sus respectivos países y, por ende, de sus culturas, tienen distintas reacciones provocadas por lo que Bloom llama la ansiedad de la influencia. Estos poemas son muestra de una manera más sofisticada e innovadora de revalorar o descontinuar con los mitos culturales de los países hispanos de los cuales Esteves y Agosin se encuentran espacialmente separadas.

El primer poema que habremos de analizar se titula "A Julia y a mí" y pertenece a la colección *Yerba Buena* de Sandra María Esteves. El texto del poema es el siguiente,

A Julia y a mí

Me fui a la obra y te vi, Julia
en tus versos caminé tu río
andé los pisos de la tierra roja
combatiendo la tierra blanca
me entregué adentro tus palabras.

but why did you let the dragon slay you
why did your vision suffocate
in suicidal promonition you could not die
within the flesh beat the heart
and my child need no image of despair
or too much poetry of this and that but not enough
to raise above the clouded cross.

Me fui, y me diste un vaso florido de ser
una hoja de verde cortada
eres mujer y mujeres muriendo
I viewed a saint and saw myself instead
in cracks of time containing the space of all
my sisters, she dances around with your words
she springs new life from your roots dried and seasoned
accidents stepping across your occult
roll along in purple hymn.

Dime, ¿cuándo llegaste a ser la eternidad del barrio?
te doy mis sueños
y cojo mi número que nunca viene de otra mano

con mi misma mano fuerte
mi carácter de ser
libertada por el viento en el ambiente social
y tú Julia?
te perdiste en palabras no en vida
you let the dragon slay you
you let life cut your sorrow from wrinkles young
you let the wine mellow your hatred
dissolving the fuel that nourished your fires of wisdom
you gave in, a breath at a time
and the eagle's wing consumed your existence

Miro tu cara, tus ojos mirando el mundo
el mismo que miraba mi madre
siento el ritmo en tu pecho, el mismo
que cubre mis canciones corriendo encima del río superficial
oigo tus versos del universo, humanidad y de mujer
it is the same world that has not moved
but an inch from your suffrage women still
tend fires that men burn
and lovers still imprison dreams
and truth remains cold like your bones

Mujer, siento el frío a que te das el gusto
de coger la vida colorosa
caí en lo duro a que reconozca el viento
amaneciendo en tu cara suave y feliz
a ti Julia, ya será tarde
pero a mí no, yo vivo
y grito si me duele la vida
y canto con la gente
y bailo con mis hijas
no soy lágrima de ser
soy el río
la mariposa y culebra
my fist is my soul
it cuts into the blood of dragons

and mark time with the beat of an Afro-cuban drum[6]

En una reciente lectura de poesía dada por Esteves en la ciudad de
Nueva York, explicó, antes de leer este poema, que asistió una noche a
una velada poética en honor a Julia de Burgos. Al salir del lugar y haber
sido enfrentada en él con la producción de su compatriota, se sintió en la
necesidad urgente de escribir un poema sobre ella. El poema escrito es
el que aquí estudiamos.

Desde el título aparece una clara intertextualidad con el poema de
de Burgos "A Julia de Burgos."[7] En este caso, además, el mismo ya
indica la intención de utlizar "A Julia" para llegar "a mí," o sea, de lo
que Bloom señala como la necesidad de "swerve away from his precursor
(Bloom, p. 14). Julia y su poesía le sirven a Esteves para llegar a sí misma

y su mundo literario, a través de su hablante.

La primera estrofa indica que la hablante siguió de primera intención los pasos de Julia: "caminé tu río." En adición, señala el haber bebido de la poesía de Julia para su propia inspiración: "me entregué adentro tus palabras." Hasta aquí, la hablante ha señalado solamente los motivos aprendidos de la poesía de Julia. La primera revisión o *swerve* ocurre cuando la hablante cambia de idioma y comienza la segunda estrofa cuestionando en tono acusativo a Julia.

Es interesante notar que esta sección acusativa aparece luego de haber señalado que había entregado "adentro tus palabras," La asimilación que ha hecho entonces la hablante de las palabras de Julia, de la poesía de la misma, ha sido un *misreading* (Bloom, p. 14). Pese a señalar la internalización, o debido a ella, le pregunta a Julia en tono de amonestación: "but why did you let the dragon slay you." La hablante ha tomado el conocimiento que tiene de la muerte de Julia por abandono propio, y lo ha leído en su poesía, de ahí que sea un *misreading*. Es cierto que Julia (de Burgos) trata el tema de la muerte casi proféticamente en algunos de sus poemas, pero la hablante del poema de Esteves va más allá y revisa ese tema para incorporar los datos de la muerte de la poeta y para apartarse de ella y de su muerte.

Julia (de Burgos) tiene dos poemas, "Dadme mi número" y "Poema para mi muerte," en los que trata ese tema. En "Poema para mi muerte" la hablante señala "Morir conmigo misma, abandonada, y sola" al comienzo, y termina con las siguientes líneas "Un clavel interpuesto entre el viento y mi sombra/hijo mío y de la muerte, me llamará poeta."[8] Nótese en la línea anterior que es la muerte de Julia (de Burgos) lo que hará que la llamen poeta. Su desintegración material dará vida a un clavel visto por el hablante de de Burgos como hijo. Es ese hijo quien le dará el nombre de poeta. Ciertamente que el clavel es símbolo de un hijo/seguidor poético. Es curioso entonces que el poema de Esteves diga: "a ti Julia, ya será tarde/pero a mí no, yo vivo/ y grito si me duele la vida/y canto con la gente/y bailo con mis hijas . . ." Estas líneas aparecen como un movimiento correctivo al poema precursor "Poema para mi muerte." Explico. La hablante del poema de Julia (de Burgos) morirá para vivir *en* su hijo (el clavel). La hablante de Esteves vivirá para bailar *con* sus hijas. La visión que la hablante de de Burgos tiene de los que seguirá a su muerte es positiva, pese a su visión negativa sobre sí misma: el clavel/hijo la llamará poeta. Por otro lado, en el poema de Esteves la hablante, pese a tener una visión más optimista sobre sí misma, vivirá, gritará, cantará, tiene una visión negativa de lo que habrá de seguirle: "and my child need no image of despair/or too much poetry of this and that but not enough/to rise above the clouded cross." La poesía no será suficiente para que el hijo en el poema de Esteves resucite (rise). Al contrario del poema de Julia (de Burgos), en el que el hijo/clavel/seguidor se levantará de la muerte de su precursora, la hablante de Esteves teme a que su hijo (child)/seguidor no pueda levantarse después de su muerte.

Bloom señala que el poeta joven o efebo comienza por rebelarse contra la consciencia de la necesidad de la muerte más que ningún otro ser humano (Bloom, p. 10). El efebo, en su intento por evitarla, cae, necesariamente, en la disminución de la poesía. En el caso de estos dos poemas, la hablante de Julia/la precursora acepta su muerte "Morir conmigo misma . . ." La hablante de Esteves/la seguidora se rebela contra la muerte, de ahí que acusa a Julia de haberse dejado matar. A la misma vez, el poema de Esteves es una disminución de la poesía, ya que el hijo (the child)/seguidor en el poema de Esteves no podrá levantarse por o debido a la poesía ("or too much poetry of this and that but not enough/to rise above the clouded cross").

El poema de Esteves no supone un cambio en énfasis de la poesía de Julia ya que los mismos temas vuelven a ser tratados, pero sí indica una continuación distinta de ellos. Bloom indica que "Heresy resulted, generally, from a change in emphasis, while revisionism follows received doctrine along a certain point, and then deviates, insisting that a wrong direction was taken at just that point, and no other (Bloom, p. 29). De ello que creamos que este poema de Esteves supone una revision y no una herejía, según indicara Barradas al estudiar este poema. Otros ejemplos en el poema de Esteves nos indican que "A Julia y a mí" es una revisión de la poesía de Julia (de Burgos):

1) Ante la indicación del poema de Julia "Dadme mi número" de que otros le señalen a la hablante el momento de morir, el poema de Esteves indica "y cojo mi número que nunca viene de otra mano/con mi misma mano fuerte." La idea es la misma—el número, ocupar su lugar en la cadena de muertes—pero la solución es distinta. En de Burgos, que otros le asignen el momento de morir; en Esteves, la hablante misma se asignará ese momento.[9]

2) En el poema "A Julia de Burgos," la hablante indica "a mí me riza el viento . . ." El poema de Esteves lee "mi carácter de ser/libertada por el viento en el ambiente social." Nuevamente, es el mismo motivo empleado: el viento. En el poema de Julia (de Burgos), el viento contorsiona, moldea, riza. En el de Esteves, desata y libera.

3) El poema "Río Grande de Loíza" de Julia termina con las líneas "¡Río Grande de Loíza . . . Río grande. Llanto grande./El más grande de todos nuestros llantos isleños,/si no fuera más grande el que de mí sale/por los ojos del alma para mi esclavo pueblo."[10] El texto de Esteves indica "no soy lágrima de ser/soy el río." El motivo del río es el mismo. Para la hablante de Julia es símbolo del llanto isleño, pero no del suyo que es mayor—es otro río. Para la hablante de Esteves no existen dos ríos, uno privativo y otro colectivo, sino uno, y ella es el río. El poema de Julia establece la

dicotomía hablante que llora y pueblo en llanto. La hablante de Esteves ve esa dicotomía, pero la une; la hablante se ve a sí misma como el río, como el llanto del pueblo.

4) El poema "A Julia de Burgos" termina con la línea "Contra ti y contra todo lo injusto y lo inhumano,/yo iré en medio de ellas con la tea en la mano." El poema de Esteves señala "my fist is my soul/it cuts into the blood of dragons." Ambos indican una postura combatiente, pero mientras la hablante de de Burgos sólo será líder (llevará la tea en la mano), la hablante de Esteves hará que su mano sea puñal, espada. Nuevamente, la revisión es obvia.

Dado todo lo observado anteriormente, podemos concluir que el poema de Esteves es lo que Bloom llama "an act of creative correction (Bloom, p. 30). La ansiedad de la influencia ha llevado a Esteves a leer en la poesía de Burgos una postura que no es lo suficientemente combativa. Ello la lleva a ir más allá de las posiciones tomadas por de Burgos en sus poemas. La hablante de Esteves dice "I viewed a saint and saw myself instead." El contemplar a Julia no sólo le facilita la visión de sí misma a la hablante sino que la lleva al auto-reconocimiento de su capacidad de ir más allá de las palabras de ella: "she dances around with your words/she springs new life from your roots dried and seasoned." Las palabras "dried and seasoned" indican cuán caduca ve la hablante de Esteves la poesía de su precursora. Esteves crea con esto el *clinamen* entre ella y de Burgos, o sea, el desvío. (Bloom, p. 14). La hablante de Esteves habrá de sacar nueva vida de las raíces secas de las palabras de Julia—irá más allá que su precursora.

El "purple hymn," que era como la hablante de Esteves describía la poesía de Julia, se torna en "the beat of an Afro-cuban drum," descripción de la poesía de Esteves misma. Si la poesía de Julia de Burgos ha sido vista tradicionalmente como estandarte de la labor creadora de la mujer comprometida en la isla en este siglo, y, por ende, como símbolo de cultura, Esteves al revisar la posición de Julia como mujer comprometida y poeta señala la manera como ambas labores pueden ser llevadas un paso más allá. La escritora *neorrican* pide en este poema su inclusión en la tradición cultural literaria puertorriqueña, representada por de Burgos, para poder llevar esa vertiente cultural más allá de los parámetros a los que ha llegado hasta ahora en la isla.

El poema "El país dividido" de Marjorie Agosin es, al igual que el texto de Esteves, metapoético. En él, la hablante se dirige a dos figuras cumbres de la cultura literaria chilena: Pablo Neruda y Nicanor Parra. La ansiedad de la influencia hace que Agosin, a través de su hablante, reduzca la estilística poética de Parra y Neruda a la inverosímil reacción que tendrían ante el robo de un objeto tan común como un calcetín. El texto a que me refiero es el siguiente,

144

El país dividido
Confieso que en La Reina,
me robé un pobre calcetín azul.
Es decir, se traspapeló.

He aquí entonces:
las verdaderas diferencias:

Pablo Neruda hubiese dicho:
Oh calcetín submarino
arrasado por la sal y
el aceite de la tierra
colgando entre el agua y el aire.

Y Nicanor Parra:
Rubia de tal por cual . . .
devuélvelo
a su Reino
unos pies hediondos. [11]

En la primera lectura del poema, el título hace pensar en la división presentada por Neruda y Parra dentro de la cultura literaria de Chile. Pero, lecturas subsiguientes nos otorgan otra visión de ese mismo título. Agosin puede con ello estar señalando hacia una descontinuidad entre su poesía y la de los dos mencionados. Esta aseveración se intensifica al observar el texto en base a lo que Bloom señala como *kenosis* y en el cual el poeta joven o efebo "seems to humble himself as though he were ceasing to be a poet" (Bloom, p. 15). La actuación de la hablante de Agosin corrobora esta afirmación. Primeramente, reduce su escritura a un robo. El acto señala la ansiedad de la influencia que la hablante de Agosin siente en relación con los poetas mencionados: su poesía (la de la hablante) podría ser vista como un robo de inspiración, una toma o apropiación de la poesía de ellos para hacerla suya. La reducción de su postura como poeta, al convertirse en una simple ladrona, se intensifica con la reducción también de lo que ha robado: un pobre calcetín azul. El calcetín traspapelado no es otra cosa que la poesía de sus precursores. Bloom señala que el efebo al humillarse ante el precursor lo hace de tal forma que "the precursor is emptied out also . . ." (Bloom, p. 15) La reducción de la poesía de Parra y Neruda a ser un pobre calcetín confirma esta aseveración. Si la hablante/poeta se humilla a ser una ladrona/seguidora, lo que roba—el calcetín/la poesía de sus precursores—queda también humillado en su reducción. Bloom afirma que 'Undoing' the precursor's strength in oneself serves also to 'isolate' the self from the precursor's stance . . ." (Bloom, p. 88). El acto de robar señala esa separación o aislamiento. Además, al deshacer la fuerza poética de Neruda y Parra, reduciéndola a un pobre calcetín, la ladrona/hablante/poeta se separa de ellos. Al rebajar el estilo distinto de ambos poetas a las "verdaderas diferencias," la hablante pone las palabras de ellos en la región de la que

Bloom llama *uncanny*. Ambas respuestas son ridículas y cargadas de ironía. Cada uno de ellos se enfrenta a los hechos de una manera distinta: Neruda se dirige al calcetín, Parra a la ladrona. Neruda, en un estilo lírico, llega a señalar el lugar en donde el calcetín se halla situado: "entre el agua y el aire." Si el calcetín es su poesía, la misma se encuentra suspendida en la nada, entre dos mundos. La hablante de Agosin obliga a Neruda a definir su poesía en términos tan risibles que socaban su postura como poeta laureado. Por otro lado, aunque la postura de Parra parece ser más 'terrenal' y menos lírica, el afán de reducir que veíamos en el trato de Neruda existe también en el de Parra. El calcetín, la poesía de Parra, ha salido o pertenece a "unos pies hediondos." Los pies pestilentes, sinécdoquicamente, substituyen a Parra el poeta. Paradójicamente, aunque el coloquialismo en el estilo de Parra parecería situarlo en un terreno más mundano y cercano al lector, la ironía en su presentación es más severa que la de Neruda y obliga al lector a retirarse o separarse del texto. Parra como poeta queda reducido a lo más ordinario: a unos malolientes pies. Con ello, el poema logra llegar a un mayor grado de reducción en la perspectiva que presenta de la poesía de estos venerables escritores.

La hablante de Agosin comienza el poema reduciendo su función como poeta al humillarse con su confesión de mísera ladrona, pero el propósito de ello es usar la misma como fuerza centrífuga que traiga a Neruda y Parra la misma humillación. La descontinuidad o ruptura, en este caso, con la tradición literaria es la característica del poema y no supone una revisión como era el caso del poema de Esteves. Bloom comenta sobre el estado de *kenosis:* "the later poem of deflation is not as absolute as it seems" (Bloom, p. 15). Ello es observable doblemente en el poema de Agosin. Primeramente, el robo del calcetín se utiliza para manipular a Neruda y Parra a asumir posturas ante un hecho tan mundano con el fin de ridiculizarles. La ironía en la construcción de sus respuestas señala hacia un nivel en el que es la hablante de Agosin quien se levanta con la última carcajada. Es ella quien ha ejecutado una ruptura con la tradición literaria chilena. En segundo lugar, nótese que en la estructura del poema la ladrona/efebo se encuentra en una posición superior a la de Neruda y Parra. Al hablar de su robo, estructuralmente se coloca al principio o encima de los poetas a quienes gradualmente irá reduciendo. La poesía de Neruda queda en un plano intermedio "colgando entre el agua y el aire." La progresión termina con la poesía de Parra reducida a "los pies hediondos." Por pura diversión el poema nos sugiere una figura humana cuya cabeza es la hablante de Agosin (en La Reina), en la mitad colgando—lírica o eróticamente—se encuentra la poesía de Neruda. Y los pies de dicha figura son los de Parra/su poesía (su Reino). Las palabras "La Reina" al principio y "el Reino" al final encierran la última intención del poema: en el reino de esos poetas, la hablante es la reina. Mediante este poema, Agosin se separa de esa tradición literaria de su país de origen reduciendo la figuras de sus poetas más ilustres al ámbito de caricaturas risibles.

Para finalizar quisiéramos sugerir que se emprendan estudios semejantes de las obras de aquellos escritores hispanos que utilizan lo metapoético en sus obras. La crítica hasta ahora ha tendido a ver sólo lo mimético-cultural en estos poetas. Ya es hora de desviarse de esa trayectoria o descontinuar nuestra asociación con esa veta crítica. La poesía de nuestros escritores hispanos en los Estados Unidos tiene la riqueza y merce ser vista a la luz de los nuevos desarrollos en la crítica literaria. Agosin y Esteves nada tienen que envidiar y sí mucho que enseñar a los nerudas, parras y de burgos de nuestras culturas literarias.

---

[1] En *Third Woman*, 1/2 (1982), pp. 40-51. Sobre la poesía de Esteves ver también en la misma revista "Consciencia femenina, consciencia social: la voz poética de Sandra María Esteves," por Efraín Barradas, pp. 31-34.

[2] Sobre la misma disyuntiva en las escritoras chicanas ver el artículo de Eliana Rivero, "Escritura chicana: la mujer," *La palabra*, 2/2 (Otoño, 1980), pp. 2-9.

[3] Efraín Barradas y Rafael Rodríguez, *Herejes y mitificadores*, (Río Piedras: Ediciones Huracán, 1980), pp. 11-30. Ver también de Barradas su artículo "De lejos en sueños verla . . .: visión mítica de Puerto Rico en la poesía neorrican," *Revista Chicano-Riqueña*, 8/4 (1979), pp. 46-56.

[4] Barradas/Rodríguez, p. 18.

[5] Harold Bloom, *The Anxiety of Influence: A Theory of Poetry* (Oxford, New York: Oxford University Press, 1973).

[6] "A Julia y a mí" en *Yerba Buena* (New York: Greenfield Review Press, 1980), p. 51. Esteves nació en los Estados Unidos de padres puertorriqueños.

[7] Julia de Burgos, "A Julia de Burgos" en *Antología poética* (San Juan: Editorial Coquí, 1977), pp. 23-24. De Burgos nació en Puerto Rico y vino a los Estados Unidos siendo adulta. Falleció en 1953.

[8] De Burgos, "Poema para mi muerte," en *Antología poética*, pp. 128-129.

[9] De Burgos, "Dadme mi número," *Antología poética*, p. 108.

[10] De Burgos, "Río Grande de Loíza," *Antología poética*, pp. 26-27.

[11] "El país dividido" en *Conchalí* (New York: Senda Nueva de Ediciones, 1980), p. 49. Ver la reseña de este libro hecha por la autora de este estudio en la *Revista de Estudios Hispánicos*, 1981.

Tey Diana Rebolledo

Abuelitas:
Mythology and Integration in
Chicana Literature

One special characteristic of the literature that Chicanas write is a concern about the family, immediate and extended. The effect of familial relationships is to be seen both in the narrative and in poetry. Mirandé and Enríquez in *La Chicana* (1979) point out that an important feature of Chicano culture is its emphasis on respect: one source being a long-standing deference to elders.[1] In the close knit family structure stretching out over several generations, *abuelitos* play an important part. Goodman and Beman (1971) report them to be seen by their grandchildren as "warm and affectionate" rather than as authority figures.[2] They are also perceived as influential rather than as powerful. Enriqueta Vásquez, when talking about her culture and beliefs, explains: ". . . I have a special place in my heart for the viejitos de nuestra raza . . . We must learn, we must study, but to memorize facts and not be able to apply them; to learn and not be able to relate to the realities of life, is criminal. It's like being castrated. Our real education, our realities and philosophies, come from our viejitos. We learn from them, we learn to apply our schooling. Our viejitos are our knowledge, and we bury it every time we bury one of our people."[3]

In surveying the texts by Chicana authors in which *abuelitos* appear, two major components emerge: 1) attitudes which link grandparents with cultural heritage and the past and, 2) the importance of these familial relationships to the writer. The intention of this paper is to examine how the positive, subjective feeling about the *abuelita* is recreated by the Chicana writer into a mythic mirror image of integration in the journey into herself.

In Chicana poetry, many texts deal with familial relationships: with mothers, fathers and siblings. Grandparents are also frequently mentioned, but the *abuelo* appears only rarely. It is the *abuelita* (note the affectionate diminuitive) who constantly surfaces in a variety of roles. This occurs perhaps because the *abuelita*, having outlived her husband, has come to live with the family or the family has gone to live with her. Or, if the *abuelo* is alive, he does not interact so intensely with his nietas. Another compelling argument may lie in the interest evidenced by Chicana writers in search of cultural roots and female role models from the past. The searching for female to female relationships to discover values, resources and coping mechanisms uncovers the various bonds granddaughters have with their grandmothers. These interfamilial dynamics symbolize the handing down of cultural traditions through the female line, establishing and affirming values. The bond functions to destroy the feeling of isolation.

It is interesting to note that mothers do not as often appear as favorably as *abuelitas* in the eyes of their daughters. Mothers function on the front line, as it were, of the family interaction and although love is often present, there is also conflict, misunderstanding and alienation. At times the mother, because she suffered deprivation, prejudice and the hardship of trying to assimilate into the dominant culture, turns her back on the values and Spanish language of her own parents. To help her children become more fully integrated, she might not allow them to speak Spanish or she might be passive about the assertion of the Spanish language as a value. She might also encourage a sense of fatalism or some non-assertive behavior on the part of her daughter. This apparent passivity on the part of the mother emphasizes the loss of identity felt under the stress of new ways. This attitude is clearly expressed in "Refugee Ship" by Lorna Dee Cervantes.

> Like wet cornstarch, I slide
> past my grandmother's eyes. Bible
> at her side, she removes her glasses.
> The pudding thickens.
>
> Mama raised me without language.
> I'm orphaned from my Spanish name.
> The words are foreign, stumbling
> on my tongue. I see in the mirror
> my reflection: bronze skin, black hair.
>
> I feel I am a captive
> aboard the refugee ship.
> The ship that will never dock.
> El barco que nunca atraca.[4]

Often it is only when the daughter is grown and the mother dead that the daughter understands what the mother tried to do for her. The antagonistic inter-relationship between mother and daughter is a difficult one and not immediately resolved. This is evident in "Baby Doll" by Rina Rocha.

> Mothers can be
>   jealous gods
> Just like
>   husbands
> Unforgiving and demanding

149

Saying
naughty girl,
naughty ought
to have done that
Naught ought
to have said that.

I rake carefully
on their grounds—
gathering my fallen
words and actions
into a neat clump.

Neat and Bitter Clump.

And I . . .
am amazed still—
at me!
That I should
wait for those
candied coated loving
words of approval
from
      jealous gods.[5]

Mothers thus function at times to stifle growth and development; they
serve as symbols of repression, of a tradition that stifles.

    Grandmothers, however, evoke a different sentiment. They often
appear in poems and short stories, at times becoming the central character in the text. Such is the case, for example, in Estela Portillo's "The
Paris Gown." In this story, Clotilde, the grandmother, tells her granddaughter Theresa how she came to live as a free, independent woman
in Paris. Brought up in a traditional household, her father decided to
marry Clotilde off to an older wealthy neighbor in order to stifle her
rebelious impulses. After a struggle, Clotilde agrees only if they buy her
a beautiful gown from Paris. The gorgeous dress arrives and the night of
her engagement party, Clotilde comes down the stairs before the assem-
bled guests stark naked. "It was simple after that. My father could not
abandon an insane daughter, but he knew that my presence meant
constant reminder. He let me come to Paris with sufficient funds . . . and
here I made my home."[6] The contrast between the Paris gown (symbolizing woman's role) and appearing naked (casting off society's rules and
regulations) dramatizes the struggle for independence. The solution to
the problem is ingenious. The role model of how to live creatively is thus
communicated to the granddaughter who is the recipient of the "object
lesson."

    For the most part *abuelitas* form a complex of female figures who
are nurturing, comforting and stable. They are linked symbolically and
spatially to the house and home, and are often associated with an

150

idealistic, cultural space of nourishment: the kitchen and the traditional Mexican foods prepared there, tortillas, chile and tamales. They provide a link to those cultural values ascribed to family, food and language. This is clearly seen in "New Year's Eve" by Rina Rocha.

> Did you seem to forget in the old
> days back in '61-'62?
> When all the aunts, grandma and you—
> Be in the kitchen making tamales?
> Some teaching their teenage daughters
> to spread masa evenly over corn
> husks.
> It was New Year's Eve
> and everyone under one roof.[7]

The extolling of the virtures of tradition and of grandmothers is also seen in "Grandmother's Ghetto" by Carmelita Grant.

> We all moved away to succeed
>   and missed ourselves
>   lodged in the hearts
>   and minds
>   of our grandparents.
>
> We all moved away to success
>   and told stories endlessly
>   to our children
>   of their Spanish heritage
>   that loved them
>   waited for them
>   in the ghetto.
>
> I wrote grandfather and asked him
>   to move from his ghetto:
>   to leave the roaches
>   and long dark hallways
>   to the landlord.
>
> And he replied:
>   "In *your* neighborhood
>   where would
>   your grandmother
>   find the masa and chiles
>   for her tamales.
>
>   and in *your* neighborhood,
>   who would know
>   she is a queen?"[8]

The closeness of the basic relationship with one's abuelita is also clearly evident in "Tortillitas pa' Naná" by Elena Guadalupe Rodríquez.

151

Cuando era niña,
grandma sat in the backyard
on crisp bright mornings
and afternoons
playing hide-and-go-seek
telling stories
best of all teaching me
how to make perfect mud pies.
As gentle winds breezed
through naná's kitchen windows
I could smell from yards away
fresh batches of flour tortillas
and homemade bread (naná's style).

I never wanted to share her
with the rest of my cousins
or even with my sisters.
Loving each moment
we'd be alone
without the confusion
of swarming nietos climbing
fruit trees like monkeys,
throwing lemons and oranges
but of all things
ripe figs and peaches
staining each other's favorite Sunday clothes
sometimes
naná's prized carnation or rose.
Even among so many children
su piel morena tostada por el sol
wrapped me with affection
and great care
as her watchful eyes gazed
from afar.[9]

Often the *abuelita* has raised the author and the reciprocal relationshp between grandmother and granddaughter has been the only buffer in a hostile world. Alma Villanueva, for example, expresses these feelings in "To Jesus Villanueva, With Love." She proudly and affectionately writes about her grandmother, remembering her foibles, her strength and her humor.

I brought you your chilis, your onions,
    your peppers.
and they'd always catch you
because you'd forget
and leave it lying open.
they'd scold you like a child
and be embarrassed like a child
silent, repentant, angry
and secretly waiting for my visit, the new
    supplies

we laughed at our secret
we always laughed
        you and I[10]

And later on;

Your daughter, my mother
told me a story I'd never
heard before:
        you were leaving Mexico
        with your husband and two
        older children, pregnant
        with my mother.
        the U.S. customs officer
        undid everything you so
        preciously packed, you
        took a sack, blew it up
        and when he asked about
        the contents of the sack,
        well, you popped it with
        your hand and shouted
        MEXICAN AIR![11]

The lyric speaker in most of these poems is a young girl, pre-adolescent perhaps, as the Chicana writer looks nostalgically towards the past, the childhood years, for meaning in the present. It is an emotional space remembered. One common theme in Chicano writing in general has been the nostalgia for a world lost, a world that signified spontaneity and comfort. The mythology of the past takes place spatially and emotionally: the past acquires enhanced meaning. These images contrast sharply with the stresses and ambiguity of today. The past then must be recorded to safeguard it, to preserve it, to re-enact it. The retelling of the text, the documenting of tradition, the creation of a myth in time past creates the history of the self, modifying and expanding it. *Abuelos* are the antepasados, the transmitters of culture. In some senses they are seen as more authentic and more valid than people and events in the present. As Evangelina Vigil succinctly states in "apprenticeship;"

I hunt for things
that will color my life
with brilliant memories
because I do believe
lo que nos dice
la mano del escritor:
that life is remembering

when I join my grandmother
for a tasa de café
and I listen to other stories
de su antepasado

153

her words paint masterpieces
and these I hang
in the galleries of my mind:

I want to be an artist like her.[12]

The documentation of the presence of the Chicana in her past reaffirms her identity. Recently, for example, there have been exhibits of photographs and films such as the exhibit on the Historical Growth of the Mexican Community in Los Angeles, one on Women and Tradition in the Bay Area and the films "Agueda Martínez" and "Traditional Perspectives": all unearth and preserve Chicano heritage through out *antepasados*.

In the lives of our *abuelos* are secrets, stories, heroic deeds and mysteries forgotten. The writer approaches them in an attempt to understand herself. Bernice Zamora writes in "Andando,"

From tomb to tomb voy andando,
buscando un punto final
to an age ya mero olvidado.

Cuando en las ruinas de Xlak-pak
hallando un tesoro de oro
explorers are less puzzled.

Than I am now on this mountain.
Con el alma del presente
yo sucumbo al pasado.

And to the secrets rolling through tall weeds
of my abuelos' mountain. I listen to their
laughter among the field mice.

From tomb to tomb voy andando
buscando un punto final
to an age ya mero olvidado.[13]

Tomás Rivera speaks of three stages he sees in Chicano literature: 1) one of conversation which records and preserves deeds and people, 2) the stage of rebellion and conflict, and 3) the stage of invention and creation.[14] It would seem at first glance that the literature about *abuelitas* would fall into the first stage of conservation: the remembrances of people that need to be recorded and preserved. Yet the importance of heritage and tradition, and the influence of whose who act as transmitters or facilitators, highlights the *abuelita* as a creator and inventor of a new mythos. *Abuelitas* serve not only as a backdrop to heritage but also as a mirror image of the past for the writer herself. Lorna Dee Cervantes is, in particular, very explicit on this issue. She admires her *abuelita* for her survival skills, for her self reliance, for her authenticity. *Abuelitas* know who they are. This myth is one which may or may not have some relationship to reality, but in the art of creation the myth is one that is imaged by the writer in the search for self. It is the feminine desire for Other: not the Other male figure, as Jung would suggest, but the Other female figure representing a degree of sameness. In "Beneath the Shadow of the Freeway" by Cervantes, the lyric speaker retraces her beginnings in search of a self she can accept. Her grandmother is wise in the ways of nature, believes in myths, is an "innocent Queen." The contrast between her "soft" *abuelita* and her mother a "fearless Warrior" points out the contrast between mother and grandmother. It is to a positive image of the *abuelita* that the granddaughter turns: to the grandmother's acceptance of body, soul and life experience, to her integrity and self-integration. The poem deals with, among other things, the relationship between men and women and Cervantes spins the golden thread that binds her to her *abuelita*.

> She likes the way of birds,
> respects how they show themselves
> in exchange for toast and a whistle.
>
> She believes in myths and birds,
> and trusts only what she has built
> with her own hands.

The lyric speaker has survived the violence engendered by men: a violence suffered by her mother and her grandmother, and looks to a future that is of her own making:

> and, in time, I will plant geraniums.
> I will tell myths about birds.
> I will tie up my hair into loose braids
> and only trust what I have built
> with my own hands. [15]

The links between Cervantes and her *abuelita* appear again in a series of poems called "Shells."

> you said
> you suffered
> a sheltered life
>
> I want to scratch
> that envy
> from your voice
>
> I take refuge
> in the fact
> that every
> pleasure

I've worked myself
like the fireplace

my grandmother built
still standing
all these years

every stone
set furiously
in place[16]

Often the grandmother exemplifies a knowledge and wisdom
identified with magic and old ways. Pat Mora connects the abuelita and
magic, imaging them to the curandera and the healing process.

Abuelita Magic

The new mother cries with her baby
in the still desert night,
sits on the dirt floor of the two-room house,
rocks the angry bundle
tears sliding down her face.

The *abuelita* wakes, shakes her head,
finds a dried red chile,
slowly shakes the wrinkled pod
so the seeds rattle

          ts . ss, ts . ss.

the *abuelita*

          ts . ss, ts . ss.

gray-haired shaman

          ts . ss, ts . ss.

cures her two children

          ts . ss

with sleep[17]

And again for Cervantes in "The Body as Braille" the image of the
grandmother is associated with female wisdom, intuition, witches and
magic. It is now fused to a moment of sexuality, a time one does not
normally associate with abuelitas.

He tells me, "Your back
is so beautiful." He traces
my spine with his hand.

I'm burning like the white ring
around the moon. "A witch's moon"
dijo mi abuela. The schools call it

"a reflection of ice crystals."
It's a storm brewing in the cauldron
of the sky. I'm in love

but won't tell him
if it's omens or
ice.[18]

These female attributes of intuition, magic and tradition and their integration are connected to the grandmother even more closely in another poem by Cervantes, "El sueño de las flores," where the journey into self, the weaving together of past and present, and the mythos created are fully and consciously explained.

> The things I remember most
> I sift through again.
>
> It's not lost because I have it
> tucked away
> somewhere behind memories
> of the Paseo de las Flores,
> la primavera when my grandmother danced,
> lifting her skirts-to hear them tell it
> she was a clear campana ringing
> in their ears.
> She was a Spanish dancer
> who had an eye for the mandolineros.
>
> Sometimes she is in my mirror:
> la mexicana who emerges con flores,
> con palabras perdidas,
> con besos de los antepasados.
>
> Somewhere in a desert of memories
> there is a dream in another language.
> Some day I will awaken
> and remember every line.
>
> And I will whisper the Spanish
> names of her lovers,
> I will dance the lost steps of her dance.
> I will find flores y flores,
> find them and adorn her.
>
> Otra vez,
> I will find them in myself again.[19]

We find no imprisoning glass images, no bell jars in this poetry. The mirror images serve to integrate the past and the present. If not dance one's own dance is an image of independence, the lyric speaker must search in the past to her grandmother to find and recuperate the lost dance. The myth of the model of the grandmother as independent, courageous and self-reliant helps establish and affirm the artist's own values. The myth of the journey to the interior will still be a journey, but the myth is not a myth lost forever, it is a journey waiting to be discovered. If the myth of the hero is one of adventure, the myth of the heroine/*abuelita* is one of determination, of integration, of finding one's own space: it is the fireplace passionately put together stone by stone, trusting no one but yourself. It is the finding of those values and ideals by yourself and in yourself. The text itself functions as the thread that links grandmothers and granddaughters. The female hero is about to be born, a heroine in a long line of heroines, nietas and abuelitas fused by a common bond: bloodline and sex. It is the myth of the integration of the female who is both courageous and womanly. The other language, once lost but now being rediscovered, is in the process of becoming: the dream will become a reality.

---

[1] Alfredo Mirandé and Evangelina Enríquez, *La Chicana*. Chicago: University of Chicago Press, 1979, 98.

[2] In Mirandé and Enríquez, 112.

[3] Enriqueta Vásquez in *Literatura Chicana: Texto y Contexto*, eds. Antonia Castañeda-Shular, Tomás Ybarra-Frausto and Joseph Sommers. Englewood Cliffs, N.J.: Prentice-Hall, 1972, 268.

[4] Lorna Dee Cervantes, *Emplumada*. Pittsburgh: University of Pittsburgh Press, 1980, 41.

[5] Rina García Rocha, *Eluder*. Chicago: Alexander Books, 1980, 20.

[6] Estela Portillo Trambley, *Rain of Scorpions*. Berkeley: Tonatiuh International, 1975, 8.

[7] Rocha, 62

[8] Carmelita Grant, *Comadre* 2 (1978), 25.

[9] Elena Guadalupe Rodríguez, *Morena*. Santa Barbara: 1980, 72.

[10] Alma Villanueva, *Bloodroot*. Austin: Place of Heron's Press, 1977, 52-53.

[11] Villanueva, 54.

[12] Evangelina Vigil, *Nade y Nade*. San Antonio: M. & A. Editions, 1978, 3.

[13] Bernice Zamora, *Restless Serpents*. Menlo Park, CA.: Diseños Literarios, 1976, 43.

[14] Tomás Rivera, "Remembering, Discovery and Volition in the Literary Imaginative Process." *Atisbos* (Summer, 1975), 66-77.

[15] Cervantes, *Emplumada*, 11-14.

[16] Cervantes, *Emplumada*, 61.

[17] Pat Mora. *Chants*, Houston: Arte Publico Press, 1984, p. 33.

[18] Cervantes, *Emplumada*, 57.

[19] Cervantes, *Mango* I:1 (1976), n.p.

Tey Diana Rebolledo

Game Theory in Chicana Poetry

Games can be divided into three groups: 1) games of physical skill, 2) games of chance and 3) games of strategy in which players are considered to be "rational players" with "rational" choices. Game theory is concerned with games of strategy only. Models for game theory include the following elements:

1) a set of decision makers or players
2) a set of strategies available to each player
3) a set of outcomes, each of which is the result of particular choices made by the players on a given play of the game
4) a set of payoffs accorded to each player in each of the possible outcomes.[1]

To these models I would include the basic decision of to play or not to play the game.

In literature when the writer mentions games, he/she is consciously symbolizing games of strategy in life using the models given above. Most often the game metaphorically describes the power struggle between men and women, but it can symbolize any power struggle. Taking this theoretical model into consideration, we will examine the Chicana writer's growing awareness of game playing as defined in her literature. Because game players are allowed to make up the rules for the game or at least to decide on the validity of the rules before playing, the feminist game player has the opportunity for changing the model before play. This change in model or rules may be seen by writers as an educational or ideal tool for changing conventional rules, espousing freedom and setting up new role models. More directly, women can be activated from passive acceptance to socially imposed roles into the recognition that she has a choice as to how the game will be played.

Games are regularized "ritual" social forms engaged in voluntarily.[2] A game is usually played in a space apart: playground, board, arena, stage, court or magic circle.[3] Special rules apply; often they are made up and accepted by the players. To play one participates in a new set of terms, rules and limits. Games, therefore, imply freedom from normal conventions or rules. They contain their own course and meaning, but, once played, the game endures as a "new found creation of the mind"; it is then transmitted and becomes a tradition of the mind.[4] Games, therefore, represent "basic values of society" and fulfill an important function for "the learning and maintenance of behavior patterns."[5] Thus, game playing and the learning of rational game strategy are important in the development of change. Often because women don't know or don't understand the rules, are unable to secure cooperation from others in the game playing or simply accept rules by which there is no chance of a positive outcome, they fail to have a positive payoff in the play. For many women options have been limited by the absence of rights, by refusal of others to cooperate in the case of activities which require such cooperation or by the normative constraints others play on their activities. It is clear that given the freedom of the player to manipulate and plan strategy within the game, the feminist author can express in her literature her growing consciousness of the power and manipulation struggle involved in games. Changing the role woman defines for herself functions as a model for change for society. Ideally, game theory should be a theory of conflict resolution rather than a theory of optimal decision in the pursuit of self interests. Women, who have often opted for "other" rather than "self," have suffered victimization and manipulation at the hands of other game players (man, society, bosses). In order to achieve conflict resolution in the form of equanimity and dialogue, feminist game players need to learn "rational" strategies in order to reach the payoff they desire.

In Latin American literature much attention has been given by literary critics to such famous male game players as Cortázar, Borges and Cabrera Infante. Little has been given to Hispanic women game players, although there are many. In another paper I studied three writers who represent various aspects of game playing.[6] Alfonsina Storni, for example, is a model of game rebellion: a woman who clearly understood the symbolic meaning of the game. The player in her poems has great freedom of choice as to whether or not she will play. Often Storni's players are on the outside, choosing not to participate because they see that in games where rules are made by men intending to victimize them, women can never win. For Storni women must become "rational" players: only by learning and using the rules, a "learned mastery" of the game, can she win. Rosario Castellanos also clearly saw the need for women to become "rational" players. She believed that once a woman understood the processes socializing her into a subordinate position, she could begin to modify the process. For Castellanos a "rational" player is defined as one able to choose consistently among the possible risky outcomes. But her position implies that women are free to take the risk. Castellanos sees the game as one of chess where both sides are equal. Although her players are free, the outcome is one of suspense. A step further, however, in the next literary generation, Elena Milán envisions game players as independent women who refuse to play the game according to masculine rules: her players set their own rules and offer an invitation to create new models and to develop new combinations.

These then are Latin American writers who deal with games and who can be seen as clearly evolving a tradition of consciously given game playing. Can we see a similar trend in Chicana literature? Chicana literature is still in its developmental state, yet in the last ten to fifteen years we have a rapidly maturing and vital body of texts to study. The use of humor and the consciousness of game playing has not yet developed into the full systems seen in Storni, Castellanos and Milán. Nevertheless, Chicana writers are very much aware of games being played and to *be* played and have explored some responses.

Chicana game players refuse to enter Macho/Don Juan games. Don Juan is the game player *par excellence* in the game between the sexes. His interest lies only in self payoff with a negative other orientation. He destroys and victimizes the unschooled female player in his path. This particular game is one Chicana players have learned to control. They are no longer an innocent, trusting Doña Inés. Educated, rational players do not look to Don Juans for a reflection of themselves. The game player in "Bus Stop Macho" by Ana Montes is approached by a Don Juan who says, "Ay mamacita, where you going/ A nice, fine looking girl like you." The woman responds,

> Hey you, Macho
> where's your head
> Times have changed
> And your sweet words are dead.
>
> I'm a woman to be loved
> Honored and Respected
> Yes
> But I'm a person too.
> A fellow fighter in a vicious struggle
> to liberate our people.
> Yes, you too.
>
> Hey brother, change your style
> Cause you see—
> There's a lot of women who think like me.[7]

Once the overt macho image is squelched, the covert one must be dealt with. To reach equality in the creation of new models is what game playing is about. Yet the struggle to become a rational player, at times, seems hopeless. Inés Hernández Tovar reflects humorously in "Chiflazones."

> I don't know which
> is more amusing
> or more absurd
> the fact that you call this love

or the fact that
I accept it as such.

     He: "The day you beat me
          at a game of pool
          I'll know we're equal."

     She: "The day you choose
          to wash the dishes
          I'll know we are."

Monogamy is not practiced
by either the culture
that rejects it
or the one that purports
to accept it.
     Quién eres tú
     pa' que me hagas
     sufrir tanto?

     Y quien soy yo
     pa' que te escriba
     poesía?.[8]

Game players recognize that often a strong opponent searches for a
weaker opponent for a certain win. In "Even," Marina Rivera warns her
opponent of her growing knowledge of strategy.

You look for her
someone you could crack
down the noseline
between the breasts
and lower see
brown organs, brown blood
brown bone even

these words you want
are a game and those of us
who have learned the game
have triangular hearts
which spin, gyrate
toward white, toward brown
toward ourselves most often
our way; to gather
edges like dry wood
make a bed, a bridge
lie on it

our lives are mouths
no matter how
the jaw placed
the teeth don't seal
they buckle here

```
we point them out
so when you point
at our lives
you get it straight.[9]
```

And María Saucedo acknowledges that if a woman feels she has no defenses, she will be defeated; she must find strength, she must continue if she is to win.

```
And la Mujer sat on
    the curve
And cried: "I am only a woman!"
    "I am defenseless and can do nothing!!"
    "Desgracia la mía ser mujer!"
Y se ahogó en sus propias
    lágrimas y self-pity.

Y encontraron su cuerpo
    cuando se secó el lago de lágrimas
Y dijeron ellos "La pobre se ahogó . . .
    ni modo. . . ."
Y siguieron caminando nodding their heads.

And La Mujer sat on
    the curve.
Y dice: "Pinche concrete curve, cala mucho!!"
    Se levantó y caminó,
    . . . se trompieza con una piedra . . .
Y dice: "Pinche piedra, me machucó el dedo!!"
    Echando madres siguió and
    she bumped into a lampost . . .
Y dice: "Pinche lampost . . . qué harto dolor me dejó!!!"

    PERO
Ella siguió y siguió. . . . . .
Llegó a la casa. . . . . .
Y se puso a hacer tortillas y Revolución.[10]
```

Miriam Bornstein Somoza equates participation in the playing of games with freedom of expression, particularly in the writing of poetry. An integral part of game concept is language. Communication, like games, is difficult to master. In order to communicate, one must accept a set of stable rules. Once these rules are mastered, communication itself may also become a game in which one can triumph.[11] Thus language, ritual and poetry can all be expressed as games. Bornstein Somoza says,

```
considero que fui parte del circo
aplaudí a lo romano ante jugadores cristianos
me divertí con gladiadores futbolistas
y la virgen de la macarena
me amarré como todos a un comercial
```

que por sólo un minuto
interrumpía mi programación
pero un día
al asesinar la mañana
con el sofocante rumor de las calles
los zumbidos de caras indiferentes
a cada paso me topé conmigo misma
ellos son yo
son yo misma
y desde entonces
me dieron ganas de ser bruja
y jugar a la vida con poemas[12]

In order to be a rational player, a woman must have a clear sense of whom she is. She must not search for her reflection or her sense of self in other players. She must also, if need be, look to others, both men and women, for cooperation in strategy planning. Alma Villanueva bases her game playing strategy on growth of self identity through a sense of connectedness with other women. In her long poem *Mother May I?*, the title refers to a children's game where the children ask the mother for directions, "Mother, may I take a giant step?", Villanueva explores the child giving birth to herself, thus becoming the mother. The process begins as play;

the pretend
place
is bed, we
lay together, you
tell me stories
about when you were
little and you were
bad, I
laugh and laugh
and we
are both 5
and no one's
the mother. we
hid from the
grown ups,

playing
- - - -
I think one time we
never switched
back and I stayed
your
mother and I stayed
bigger and I stayed
stronger, to take
care of you,
mother, we

forgot the world is bigger than
our bed. [13]

Once the birthing has taken place, self knowledge gives the child the
ability to play strategy, to make choices. The child is ready:

mother, may I?

don't mistake my reassuring
words
for wisdom;
don't mistake my soothing
eyes
for peace,
we are
in such a large large
world
I've
learned the ropes
I've
cultivated my gardens
I've combed my shores
I've
played house
played god
created universes
in my kitchen
in my womb
and when I
hide I
play mother
to my own little girl. I
was always
good at
make believe. all
I ask is
        may
I play? [14]

Like the poets who preceded her, Margarita Cota-Cárdenas is
clearly aware of the loss of innocence necessary to play games in society
and the need for women to put forth their own rules of the game.
Cota-Cárdenas' lyric speakers are often children playing games in their
imagination. These games serve to keep the boogy man away: that is,
they form a protective device against the real world. The self within
needs to be nurtured, so the game players resort to "pretend" games
creating another more manageable and sustaining environment. Thus,
as Huizinga states, "the child is making an image of something different,
something more beautiful or more sublime or more dangerous than
what he usually is." [15] The child is thus free to create a more satisfactory
world. As the child can "pretend," so can the adult change her world

into a desired one using the same methods. This is the case in "Mejor fingimos," by Cota-Cárdenas;

> que chiste
> > tener que morir un poeta
> > > para ser apreciado
> por qué no jugamos
> > cierra tú los ojos
> > > y yo
> > > > me acuesto aquí
> > > y al ratito
> > > > como en la Biblia
> > > > > me levanto.[16]

In addition, for Cota-Cárdenas, the adult game player must not participate in a game she defines as one-sided or in which she has no choice, even if it means her own destruction. In "Soliloquio travieso," she says,

> mucho trabajo   ser flor
> > a veces
> > > solitas
> > > > > y en camino
> concentramos muy fuerte   así
> > arrugamos la frente
> > > para marchitarnos antes
> y al llegar al mercado   ji ji
> > no nos pueden vender[17]

The implicit mischievousness implies that this player has deliberately chosen the role of "spoil sport" ruining the "payoff" for her opponent. For this game the strategy chosen (to be a withered flower and not a beautiful one) gives her on the one side a "negative payoff" in that she grows old and withered, but for her own inner self it has been a positive payoff. She remains true to her own values. This, then, is the true test of the game: the true mastery. If you can play handling the illusions, the strategic trickery of the other players, and if you master the idiom or language of the game, you are truly a rational player. To master the language of the game seems to indicate de-mythifying the traditional values and myths perpetuated by society in order to give a player a chance. The de-mythification of the opponent and a correct assessment of his true power is an important element in this game transcendence leading to new action alternatives. In "Justo Será," Cota-Cárdenas states;

> días   semanas   meses
> > sin saber de
> > > poetizados espasmos
> > todo por creer
> > > en los caballeros-andantes

        aquel pinchi bato
    y su mitificado horse
        coming down the camino-brick-road
        with a mecate-rope
        around his pescuezo-neck
    que nunca
        nunca
        llega[18]

The new role model is explicitly delineated by all these feminist game players as a rational player who makes rational choices having demythified her opponents and operating within a sphere of freedom. To begin, the rules of the game must make the players equal. If not, the players have two choices: 1) they may choose not to play or 2) they may manipulate men in the ways *women* have been manipulated in the past. Manipulation, however, is not seen as a positive value in this game playing, since it perpetuates values not adhered to by feminist game players. Rather, they are striving for direct confrontation and communication. Games require application, knowledge, skill, courage, strength and endurance. Once a woman acquires these, she can then make her own decisions as to whatever payoff she considers of value. Feminist game players traditionally do not want to concern themselves only with their personal payoffs, but rather to engage in a focus of self *and* other where the self will not be betrayed because she has been unable to play the game.

The elements that feminist game players need to master are the following: 1) demythification of the opponent; 2) support of other feminist game players to be used later in large cooperative confrontations; 3) becoming "rational" in the understanding of the ways in which women are manipulated; 4) searching for the ideal, but also equal combinations of self and other; and 5) remaining true to your own self even if the payoffs are destruction; or 6) remaining outside of the game. As Cota-Cárdenas has stated;

        busca tu nombre
        dentro de ti misma
    Chicana
        crea tu propia palabra
        tu esencia   TU

    sé homenaje a tu raza crea tu propio cosmos
    CHICANA   HERMANA   MUJER
        Ahora actúa por
            TI[19]

---

    [1] Lüchen, Günter, ed. *The Cross-Cultural Analysis of Sport and Games*. Champaign, Illinois: Stipes Publishing Co., 1970, 100.

[2] Huitzinga, J. *Homo Ludens. A Study of the Play Element in Culture*. London: Hunt Barnard and Co., Ltd., 1950, 7-8.

[3] Huitzinga, 10.

[4] Huitzinga, 10.

[5] Lüchen, 8-9.

[6] Rebolledo, Tey Diana. "Game Theory: A Typology of Feminist Players in Latin American Poetry." Paper presented at the National Hispanic Feminist Conference. San Jose, California, 1980.

[7] Montes, Ana. "Bus Stop Macho," *Comadre* (1977) 1:1, 24-25.

[8] Tovar, Inés Hernández, "Chiflazones" *Con Razón, Corazón*, 18.

[9] Rivera, Marina. "Even," in *The Third Woman: Minority Women Writers in the United States*. Ed. Dexter Fisher. Boston: Houghton Mifflin, 1980, 408.

[10] Saucedo, María. "Sobre la liberación de la mujer," in *Fiesta in Aztlan*. Santa Barbara: Capra Press, 1982, 112.

[11] Blake, Kathleen. *Play, Games and Sport*. Ithaca: Cornell University Press, 1974, 65.

[12] Bornstein-Somoza, Miriam. "Para el consumidor," in *Siete Poetas*. Tucscon, Arizona: Scorpion Press, 1978, 6.

[13] Villanueva, Alma. *Mother, May I?* Pittsburgh, Pennsylvania: Motheroot, 1978, 11-12.

[14] Villanueva, 36-37.

[15] Huitzinga, 13-14.

[16] Cota-Cárdenas, Margarita. *Noches despertando en conciencias*. Tucson, Arizona: Scorpion Press, 1975, n.p.

[17] Cota-Cárdenas, n.p.

[18] Cota-Cárdenas, n.p.

[19] Cota-Cárdenas, n.p.

The American Association of Teachers of Spanish and Portuguese

Richard B. Klein, Secretary-Treasurer
Holy Cross College
Worcester, Massachusetts 01610

FIFTEEN DOLLARS PER YEAR DUES INCLUDE AATSP MEMBERSHIP AND HISPANIA SUBSCRIPTION

BOOK REVIEW EDITOR
Myron I. Lichtblau
Dept. of Rom. Langs
Syracuse Univ.
Syracuse, NY 13210

EDITOR
Donald W. Bleznick
Dept. of Rom. Langs
Univ. of Cincinnati
Cincinnati, OH 45221

ADVERTISING MANAGER
Albert R. Turner
Glenbrook South H S
4000 W. Lake Ave
Glenbrook, IL 60025

Julia Ortiz Griffin

The Puerto Rican Woman in René Marqués' Drama

René Marqués is probably, after Hostos, the best known of all Puerto Rican authors, and certainly his country's leading playwright. Profoundly concerned with the problems of Puerto Rico, he made them the substance of his dramas. He saw these problems arising from the abandonment of cultural traditions and values, and traced them to the industrialization and modernization that transformed the island under the domination of the United States. His work constantly affirms the need for self-respect and the assertion of identity; no where is this more evident than in the presentation of the Puerto Rican woman in his dramas.

Under "Operation Bootstrap" foreign businesses and investments were attracted to the island during the 1950s and 1960s by tax exemptions and the promise of cheap labor. Hundreds of factories were established, tens of thousands of industrial workers were employed, new roads, housing developments and shopping complexes were created; a tremendous increase in annual production, average income and standard of living were attained. The government thus changed the face of Puerto Rico, and, within little more than a decade, the island was transformed from the "Poorhouse of the Caribbean" into a country with the highest per-capita income in Latin America. But this economic miracle had serious social implications. A people accustomed over many generations to a slow-moving, tradition-bound way of life had been industrialized, urbanized and plunged into the preoccupations of a technological age. Once largely self-sufficient, almost overnight they had become consumers, obsessed with the acquisition of material goods and dependent upon government agencies and foreign investors for the satisfaction of their needs.

The Puerto Ricans, uprooted, restless, grasping at the gaudy novelties of the moment, were in danger of losing their individuality, of becoming mere cogs in the world-wide industrial complex.

This disrupted, disoriented society is the focal point of Marqués' drama. His plays are an exhortation to his people to resist the national and personal corruption of soul-less "progress." Nowhere is this appeal to identity and integrity more evident than in his numerous striking portrayals of women.

For centuries the education and indoctrination of Puerto Rican

169

women had stressed passivity and obedience as the primary virtues, synonymous with femininity.[1] A modern Puerto Rican writer who describes a female character this way: "Camelia . . . dotada de una femeneidad perfecta . . . pasiva, sentimental e intuitiva," is merely expressing an accepted concept.[2] Women eventually accepted this way of thinking. For them, too, femininity which meant passivity became the ultimate perfection of womanhood.

These women, of Puerto Rico, bred to be submissive and self-effacing, were even more profoundly threatened than their men by the great change sweeping over the island. Conditioned to a dependent status and an existence centering on the family and the home, they saw their secure way of life crumbling. As their men struggled for survival in a rapidly shifting economy, the women seemed doomed to the role of onlookers and victims. The land-oriented traditional culture was under assault by a new materialism in which the factory replaced the plantation and the farmer became an urban slum dweller. This alien and hostile environment was particularly traumatic for women, who had to abandon their almost child-like passivity and become mature human beings almost overnight. The insecurity and pain of an accelerated adolescence were the particular burden of Puerto Rican women during this turbulent period of social change.

With keen perception Marqués recognized that the national crisis which his country was undergoing affected its women in a particularly acute way. Thus the female characters of his plays, in their efforts to assert their identity and their human dignity, are the most striking embodiments of his persistent theme: the salvation of the nation's soul.

Marqués' awareness of the Puerto Rican woman's condition and burden inspired him to create very intriguing and intense female characters. They are of three distinct types. To the first belong those who are pillars of strength, sure of themselves and their values. Doña Gabriela of *La carreta (The Oxcart)* and Doña Isabel of *La muerte no entrará en palacio (Death Shall not Enter the Palace)* are such women. To the second belong those who, lacking the strength of the first type, become victims of their surroundings. Juanita of *La carreta* and Mercedes of *Un niño azul para esa sombra (A Blue Child for that Shadow)* are such. To the third belong those who, after being victims themselves, forcefully strike back and eventually prevail because of their will to do so. Casandra of *La muerte no entrará en palacio*, Micaela of *La casa sin reloj (The House Without a Clock)*, Sara of *Sacrificio en el monte Moriah (Sacrifice at Mount Moriah)* and the three old women in *Los soles truncos (The Fanlights)* are such women.

Doña Gabriela, the widowed mother in *La carreta*, is strong, the result of a life of hard work and belief in tradition and common sense. She has deep faith in a land-centered culture which eventually saves her and her remaining family. She is also, and above all, a mother. Her moves to the slums in San Juan and ultimately to New York are motivated by her concern for her children's happiness. Her son Luis rejects the rural life and is convinced that salvation lies in industrialization, in the guts of the machine—in which he, ironically, finds death. But his mother cannot defy him, not only because she loves him dearly, but because she lives by the old codes and will not oppose his decisions as head of the family.

Doña Gabriela believes that the land is the only sure and decent source of life. This conviction and her belief in moral values are out of place in the slums of San Juan and New York to which the family's wonderings take them. In San Juan she is beset by noise, stench and dirt. She complains, in the idiom of the *jíbaro:*

> ¡Tengo un dolor de cabesa . . .! ¡Lah pehteh! ¡Loh ruido! Ni la mar qué llevárseloh. Condená mar. El aire se encucia y jase daño. Pa qué silve tanta agua si no pué limpiar ehta porquería[3]

She is nostalgic for the clean air of her former home: "Era limpio el aire de la montaña."[4] Dirt is everywhere and even in the lives of all the slum dwellers. This spiritual pollution soon harms her children, victims of forces she can not control or understand—economic disruption, population shifts, unemployment, urban crime. Chaguito becomes a thief and suffers imprisonment. Juanita is raped and endures an abortion that makes her try to commit suicide. Doña Gabriela, who has been concerned about Chaguito's childish pranks and vigilant over Juanita's virtue, has to endure now the sorrow and humiliation of dishonor. Their misfortunes prompt her, in a moment of desperation, to say: "¿Por qué Dioh se está orviando e nojotroh?"[5]

It seems that God has indeed forgotten the poor *jíbaro* family. In New York, the last stop of their journey, tumult and squalor overwhelm Doña Gabriela, who must also endure the near-destruction of her family. Luis has become preoccupied with machines, and, as his sister points out, they have become his friends, his family, his whole life.[6] Doña Gabriela suffers because she sees him become more and more obsessed and unhappy: "Ehtá enfermo por dentro . . . un gusanillo de pena le ehtá royendo el corazón."[7] Moreover, she sees that Juanita has changed. She has seen her wearing make-up, curling her hair and wearing flashy clothes. But more importantly, she has seen her change her values and way of life. Juanita had moved out of their home, and, defying family honor and values, has become a prostitute. Doña Gabriela therefore realizes that the quest for happiness which brought them to a strange place with strange people who speak an incomprehensible language has failed completely. What can she do about it? While Luis is alive there is nothing much she can do. Since she will not defy the head of the family, she is forced to sit both literally and symbolically in the rocking chair the family brought from their old home. As someone says: "De atráh palante. Y de alante patráh. Moviéndose sin moverse. Moviéndose, pero sin llegar a ninguna parte."[8]

But she never loses faith, and her determination gives her strength, and her strength saves her remaining family. Her belief in the life-giving power of the land "La tierra es sagrá" which never left her, now guides her back to where she and her family truly belong.[9]

Doña Isabel, in *La muerte no entrará en palacio* (which is set in an imaginary country clearly based on Puerto Rico) is another strong woman like Doña Gabriela. She is a very level-headed person who is not deceived by outward appearances of happiness even though they may come accompanied by material prosperity and progress. She is married to a loving husband who also is a leader who has stirred their country to material prosperity and has a daughter who is sweet, affectionate and lively; moreover she lives in a beautiful island which is making tremendous progress in the field of social justice and economic development. But she is neither complacent nor satisfied, because certain values which she holds very dear are being forgotten or disregarded. She is an idealist who believes in freedom, especially freedom to live one's own destiny and use one's own resources. She cannot accept the betrayal of her people by a government, headed by her husband, that has promised bread, land and liberty, only to deliver the first at the expense of the other two. This situation, which was similar to that created by the government of Luis Muñoz Marín in Puerto Rico, confused and changed life for the people. Doña Isabel cannot accept such betrayal, and dares call her husband tyrant.[10] Though she believes in the unquestioned authority of the head of the family, like Doña Gabriela (as proven by her advice to her daughter to follow her man blindly and make his beliefs hers), she also believes that certain values, like "tierra" and "libertad" are worth fighting for. The fact that she does not put her beliefs into action can be explained by her loyalty to her husband or by the fact that her daughter, as will be seen, is driven to act first.

Marqués' female characters of the second type also suffer from the social dislocation and cultural shock caused by the new and alien materialistic spirit of the times, but do not have the strength or nobility of Doña Gabriela or Doña Isabel. They become victims of these new social forces and emerge from the experience profoundly changed. Juanita, Doña Gabriela's daughter, and Mercedes of *Un niño azul* are, though in different ways, examples of such women.

Life in the slums is not to Juanita's liking from the very beginning. Being a sensitive person, she does not adjust to it or accept it. She protests:

> ¿Qué tú te creeh? ¿Que voy a ehtar tó el día viendo y oliendo la
> porquería en que vivimoh, ah? Pueh no me da la gana bay . . . Aquí to
> apehta a mierda y a basura.[11]

She seeks escape from this misery and the only kind available to her is the escape of the mind. So she spends all her time listening to soap operas on the radio and then dreams about their heroines—beautiful princesses and countesses with palaces, elegant clothes, expensive perfumes and "jabla fina" (refined speech).[12] She also dreams of a clean and decent life away from the slums, which makes her share at one point Luis' vision of moving to New York, because the snow in that city is pure and clean and it will bring purity and cleanliness to their lives. In her mind cleanliness and snow go together.

In the slums Juanita is brutally raped and has to endure the trauma of an abortion she does not believe in and that is a sin according to her religious and traditional principles. She afterwards tries to commit suicide out of shame and desperation. Though the attempt fails, the old Juanita dies that day. She becomes someone stripped of everything decent, of every dream and every value, and even of memories. Juanita the prostitute who lives in New York has escaped from her misery by means of rebelling against the old Juanita and everything she had believed in.

When at the end of the play she decides to go back with her mother to the land they left and live as the old *jíbora* family was meant to do, she is going back to her own roots. Now she and her mother share once more the same values. The difference between the two women is that Juanita has learned the hard way that true happiness can only be found in being true to oneself and to one's own traditional values and roots.

Mercedes of *Un niño azul*, like Juanita, has been hurt and changed by a hostile and materialistic society. Although her change is not as dramatic or drastic as Juanita's because she had always lacked strong desires or convictions, it is more deadly. Juanita hurts only herself by her actions, while Mercedes destroys her husband and child. Mercedes was young and weak and could not resist society's pressures to repudiate her husband's belief in freedom and way of life. Since he was imprisoned for his political beliefs and was not there to give her the strength and support she needed, she decided to join the rest of the world which for the upper class to which she belonged meant complete rejection of values that cannot be bought or sold or measured. Not only does she forget her absent husband and take a lover, but she destroys her husband's writings, which amounts to destroying his thoughts and his ideas. This is done to appease the forces of materialism represented by her banker brothers. And she destroys her little boy as well, because he adores his father and the idea of freedom for which he sacrificed his life.

Mercedes is callous and selfish, but she is also a victim. One can see that she tries to make her husband and son happy. When her husband returns home from prison, she abandons the lover for whom she still cares; she brings children to play with her little boy. But these attempts fail. She cannot establish a genuine human relationship with

173

either of them because her sensibilities have been blunted by the unfeeling ambience in which she has lived for so long.

Marqués' female characters of the third group are neither mere figures of endurance nor hapless pawns, but women who take strong action against the social forces that beset them. They are prepared to go to great lengths and make great sacrifices in order to survive and be saved. The heroines of *La muerte no entrará en palacio*, *La casa sin reloj*, *Sacrificio en el monte Moriah* and *Los soles truncos* must kill in order to save themselves from evil or corruption, to save their values or what is good and just.

Casandra, the true heroine of *La muerte no entrará en palacio*, is at first an average girl. But she is also an intense young woman, not completely frivolous. She is very much in love, and through love she finds both sacrifice and greatness. Her sweetheart's ideal of freedom and his concern over the betrayal of this ideal by her father, the governor, become hers. When she suspects the young man of planning to assassinate her father, she attempts to snatch away his gun and accidentally kills him. Moved by remorse and a new-found idealism, she then assumes his mission and sets out to destroy tyranny and the tyrant, her father. At first a product of her environment, Casandra changes through love to become a woman of high ideals. She is Marqués' model Puerto Rican, who not only believes in a cause, but is willing to sacrifice herself for it.[13]

The same change takes place in Micaela of *La casa sin reloj*, a play whose deliberate absurdity does not deprive its character of significance. At the start of the play, Micaela is living in a sort of moral limbo where her concerns are washing clothes, cleaning the house, listening to the radio and reading romantic novels. She is a product of her environment—no lofty feelings, passions or ideas, and, as she says, "sin remordimientos, conciencia o culpa."[14] She is not moved by the struggle for freedom taking place in her country nor has she felt any guilt over the oppressive conditions which beset it. In order to feel something, to feel guilty at last, she kills her brother-in-law, the only man she has ever truly loved. Whether the killing is intentional or accidental is not clear, but nonetheless, it is evident that only through violent rejection of the status quo and through sacrifice can sensitivity and conscience flourish.

Something similar happens in *Sacrificio en monte Moriah*, a play based, though quite loosely, on the biblical story of Abraham. In Marqués' play, Sara, Abraham's wife, is the central character of the drama. Sara has been forced to live a life without honor. Her husband, a stupid, tyrannical and fanatical man, has forced her to forsake her religion and to prostitute herself so that he can obtain material goods or political advantages. Though he poses as a great leader, it is because of Sara's forced involvement with the Pharoah and with another leader that Abraham has obtained his advantages. But since Abraham's meanness is accompanied by stupidity, Sara manipulates him in order to thwart tyranny and death. She makes her old husband believe that he has sired two sons, Ismael and Isaac, even though he is really impotent. When Abraham is going to sacrifice Isaac because of what he understands to be a command from his God, Sara, disguised as an angel, stops Abraham as he is about to strike the fatal blow. Finally she kills Abraham in order to free herself and the people from his tyranny. Because of her intervention, evil and superstition have been defeated. She is never afraid to act when action is needed, and therefore she can control her destiny and events.

The three old women in *Los soles truncos* are not afraid to act, either. They see their enemies, time and society, closing in on them, and they take charge of their own fate to prevent these hostile forces from destroying their old, beautiful world. They had grown up in a world where art, music and beauty were appreciated. But after the American invasion, the world that they knew and loved, together with their own youth and wealth, ceased to exist, and they had sought refuge in their own old house in San Juan. In the play, they become aware that the outside world is going to invade their sanctuary; the house is going to be taken away from them for non-payment of taxes. Rather than giving in and have their sanctuary desecrated, and being forced to live in a time and world that is not theirs, they set fire to the house and perish in a glorious suicide.

Casandra, Micaela, Sara and the three old women are brave women who see the need for action and sacrifice to right wrongs. The fact that they resort to crimes in order to accomplish their noble aims is not as important as the message that acquiescence, status quo or complacency are not solutions to the problems of having to live in a materialistic society where virtue and freedom are not valued and where women must accept corruption to survive. The only proper response to the problems is action—true, decisive action for freedom and the ideal.

René Marqués tells us what happens when there is no action or dedication. It is the world of *El apartamento*. The world of its heroine can become the world of the Puerto Rican woman if she chooses material goods and practical or expedient solutions over virtue and freedom. In this play, Carola does not have to worry about cooking or cleaning—every need has been taken care of. But she is trapped in an apartment with no exit and is not allowed to pursue her beauty and poetry. Instead, she must devote herself to the mindless pasttime of measuring over and over a ribbon that never ends. The message is clear: if the Puerto Rican woman chooses a way of life that values material comfort above all else, she will end up like Carola in a hermetically sealed world, pursuing mindless occupations which lead to a life without intellect or sensitivity.

On the basis of some of his short stories, Marqués has earned a reputation as a misogynist. Whatever he may appear to say elsewhere, however, in his dramas he has given ample evidence of his sympathy and admiration for the Puerto Rican woman. Marqués' heroines are bursting with life and energy. Through them Marqués shows the Puerto Rican woman's position in her milieu, her strengths and her weaknesses. Most importantly, he shows how she must act and live if she is to save herself and, in so doing, her homeland.

[1] Federico Ribes Tovar, *La mujer puertorriqueña* (New York: Plus Ultra, 1972), p. 18.

[2] Pablo Morales Otero. *Cuentos y leyendas del Toa* (San Juan: Biblioteca de Autores puertorriqueños, 1968), p. 17.

[3] René Marqués. *La carreta* (Rıo Piedras: Editorial Cultural, 1963), p. 63.

[4] *Ibid*. p. 63.

[5] *Ibid*. p. 110.

[6] *Ibid*. p. 131.

[7] *Ibid*. p. 159.

[8] *Ibid*. p. 86.

[9] *Ibid*. p. 171.

[10] René Marqués. *La muerte no estrará en palacio, Teatro*, I (Rıo Piedras: Editorial Cultural, 1970), p. 276.

[11] René Marqués. *La carreta*. p. 80.

[12] *Ibid*. p. 62.

[13] Eleanor Martin. *René Marqués* (Boston: Twayne Publishers, 1979), p. 91.

[14] René Marqués. *La casa sin reloj, Teatro*, (Rıo Piedras: Editorial Cultural, 1971), p. 22.

Contributors

Achy Abejas, a native of Cuba, is a freelance writer formerly with the *Chicago Sun-Times*. Her poetry has appeared in *Cardinal, Antigonish Review* and numerous other journals.

Margorie Agosin was born in Bethesda, Maryland, and raised in Santiago, Chile. She is an associate professor of Spanish at Wellesley College. Among her publications are three books of poetry: *Chile, Conchalí* and *Silencio que se deja oír*.

Naomi Lockwood Barletta resides in Norwood, Massachusetts. She is the author of two books: *Sueños y señales* (1979) and *Fair Poetry* (1981).

Santa Barraza resides in Austin, Texas, where she teaches art and runs an art gallery.

Cordelia Candelaria is an assistant professor in the Department of English and the Chicano Studies Program at the University of Colorado at Boulder. Her poems have appeared in the *Rocky Mountain Review, RiverSedge, Grito del Sol, Rendezvous* and *Revista Chicano-Riqueña*.

Ana Castillo is a Chicana writer who resides in Chicago. She is the author of two chapbooks, *Otro Canto* and *The Invitation*, as well as of *Women are Not Roses*, a new book published by Arte Publico Press.

Sandra Cisneros is a Chicana poet and prose writer who resides in Chicago. She is the author of *Bad Boys*, published by Mango Press and *The House on Mango Street*, published by Arte Publico Press. In Winter 1982-83, Ms. Cisneros was resident poet at the Michael Karolyi Artists Foundation in Vence, France. She was also the recipient of a Fellowship for Creative Writers, 1981-82, awarded by NEA.

Judith Ortiz Cofer, a native of Puerto Rico, is a lecturer in the English Department at the University of Miami at Coral Gables. She has authored two chapbooks entitled *Latin Women Pray* and *The Native Dancer*. Her poetry has appeared in a number of journals, among these *Kansas Quarterly, Southern Humanities Review, Southern Poetry Review* and *Bilingual Review*.

Angela De Hoyos resides in San Antonio where she works as an editor/publisher with M&A Editions and as editor of *Huehuetitlan*, a Chicano literary journal. She is the author of three books of poetry: *Selections, Arise Chicano! And Other Poems* and *Chicano Poems: For the Barrio*.

Sandra María Esteves, a native of New York City, of Puerto Rican and Dominican parents, is the Artistic Director of the African Caribbean Poetry Theatre and the author of the book *Yerba Buena* (Greenfield Review Press) and numerous poems published in such magazines as *Revista Chicano-Riqueña, Sunbury 10, The Next World* and *Vórtice*. The holder of a master's degree from the Pratt Institute, her graphics have been exhibited extensively.

Roberta Fernández is a native of San Antonio whose stories have appeared in English and Spanish in the *Massachusetts Review, Tin Tan* and *Revista Chicano-Riqueña*. She is a lecturer in Women's Studies at the University of Massachusetts.

Carmen Lomas Garza, a native of Kingsville, Texas, resides in San Francisco where she is currently working on eight paintings on the "History of Northern California Water," commissioned by the City and County of San Francisco and the San Francisco Water Department. Her art work has been published in *American Women Artists, Chicano Voices, The Gypsy Wagon* and *El Grito*.

Judith Ortiz Griffin teaches at St. John's University in Jamaica, New York.

Nicholasa Mohr is the author of *Felita* (Dial Press, 1979), *In Nueva York* (Dial Press, 1977), *El Bronx Remembered* (Harper & Row, 1975), *Nilda* (Harper & Row, 1973) and the forthcoming Arte Publico Press book, *Rituals of Survival*. She is the recipient of *The New York Times* Outstanding Book, American Library Association "Best Book for Young Adults" and many other awards.

Pat Mora resides in El Paso and is the author of *Chants*, a first book of poems published by Arte Publico Press. Her poetry has been published widely in such reviews as *Amphora Review, The Bilingual Review, New America, The Pawn Review* and *Revista Chicano-Riqueña*.

Tawese O'Connor resides in Houston, Texas.

Antonia Quintana Pigno, is a native of Albuquerque, whose poetry has been published in a number of journals, among these *The Latin American Review, Rocky Mountain Review, Encore, Southwest: A Contemporary Anthology* and *La Confluencia*.

Mary Helen Ponce, A native of Pacoima, California, is an instructor with the Chicano Studies Program at California State University and a doctoral student in History at UCLA. Her works have been published in *La Opinión, Chismearte, Hispanic Link, Caminos, La Gente, El Popo* and *Corazón de Aztlán*.

Tey Diana Rebolledo teaches in the Department of Foreign Languages at the University of Nevada at Reno. She is working collaboratively with Iliana Rivero on a critical anthology of Chicana literature.

Iliana Rivero, a native of Cuba, is a professor of Spanish at the University of Arizona at Tucson. She is the author of *De Cal y Arena* and *Cuerpos Breves*. Her works have appeared in many publications, including *Alaluz, Inscape, Mester, Revista Chicano-Riqueña,* the *Denver Quarterly* and the *International Poetry Review.*

Patricia Rodríguez resides in San Francisco where she creates "Objects and Apparitions." Her masks and sculptures have been exhibited widely.

Yvonne Sapia is a resident poet at Lake City Community College in Lake City, Florida. Her manuscript, *The Fertile Crescent,* won the 1983 Anhiga Press Florida Chapbook Award.

Carmen Tafolla, a native of San Antonio resides in Austin, Texas. Her latest work, *Curandera,* was published in Spring of 1983 by the Mexican American Cultural Center of San Antonio. Ms. Tafolla's poetry has appeared in literary publications throughout the Southwest, including *Revista Chicano-Riqueña, Tejidos, Emplumece, Canto al Pueblo, Floricanto* and *Caracol.*

Luz Maria Umpierre is a native of Puerto Rico and is currently an assistant professor of Spanish at Rutgers University. She has published two collections of poetry: *Una puertorriqueña en Penna* and *En el país de las maravillas* (Third Woman Press).

Rima de Vallbona, a native of San Jose, Costa Rica, is a professor of Spanish at the University of St. Thomas in Houston. In addition to two books of literary criticism, the writer has published four books of prose: *Noche en vela, Polvo del camino, La Salamandra rosada* and *Mujeres y agonías.* Her latest work, *Las sombras que perseguimos* is currently at press.

Evangelina Vigil is the recipient of the 1983 American Book Award for her book, *Thirty An' Seen A Lot,* published by Arte Publico Press. She is the author of *Nade y Nade,* a chapbook published by M&A Editions of San Antonio. Ms. Vigil received a Fellowship for Creative Writers for 1979-80 from the National Endowment for the Arts. Presently she is completing work on her new book, *The Computer is Down,* to be published by Arte Publico Press in the Winter of 1984.

Helena María Viramontes resides in East Los Angeles. She is a widely published prose writer whose stories have won awards from *Statement Magazine* at California State University and the University of California-Irvine Chicano Literary Contest.

Silviana Wood is an actress and writer from Tucson, Arizona. She is a graduate student in Creative Writing at the University of Arizona and a drama instructor at Pima Community College.